The Collections of the Royal Geographical Society (with IBG) were used to research some of the details in this book. It is stimulating to see them used in such an inspirational way. The book should encourage children of all ages to find out more about the world they live in and how it is formed.

GEOGRAPHY HAS NEVER BEEN SUCH FUN BEFORE!

Judith Mansell – Education Officer, Royal Geographical Society

FREAKY PEAKS

ANITA GANERI

Illustrated by
Mike Phillips

Hippo

Also available:

Violent Volcanoes
Odious Oceans
Stormy Weather
Raging Rivers
Desperate Deserts
Earth-shattering Earthquakes
Freaky Peaks
Bloomin' Rainforests
Perishing Poles

Two books in one:
Raging Rivers and Odious Oceans

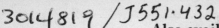

Scholastic Children's Books,
Commonwealth House, 1-19 New Oxford Street,
London WC1A 1NU, UK
a division of Scholastic Ltd
London ~ New York ~ Toronto ~ Sydney ~ Auckland
Mexico City ~ New Delhi ~ Hong Kong

First published in the UK by Scholastic Ltd, 2001

Text copyright © Anita Ganeri, 2001
Illustrations copyright © Mike Phillips, 2001

ISBN: 0 439 99873 5

Typeset by TW Typesetting
Printed and bound by Nørhaven Paperback, Viborg, Denmark

10

The right of Anita Ganeri and Mike Phillips to be identified as the author and illustrator
of this work resepectively has been asserted by them in accordance with the Copyright, Designs
and Patents Act, 1988.

CONTENTS

INTRODUCTION

Like everything else in life, geography has its ups and downs.
Take lessons about monstrous mountains, for instance. One
minute you're sitting at your desk, your head in the clouds,
daydreaming about being famous, while your geography
teacher drones on and on. . .

Next thing you know, your dreams are shattered. Your
teacher's voice brings you down to Earth with a bang. Yep,
it's all downhill from now on.

Where on Earth are you going?

* Oro-jen-ee is the technical term for the way freaky peaks are formed. It comes from two old Greek words for "mountain" and "born". In other words, your teacher's telling you you've got a mountain to climb. Don't freak out. If even climbing out of bed in the morning makes you go wobbly and weak at the knees, why not try this impressive-sounding excuse. Put up your hand, look peaky, and say:

PLEASE MISS, MY MUM SAYS I'M ACROPHOBIC** MAY I BE EXCUSED?

IT'S HIGH TIME I HAD A WORD WITH YOUR MUM

** Being acrophobic (ak-row-foe-bick) means being scared of heights. It comes from another old Greek word for "peaky" or "high up". And the freaky Greeks knew all about peaks. After all, they lived in one of the hilliest places on Earth.

If, on the other hand, you're the sort of person who thinks climbing mountains sounds dead exciting but you can't be bothered to go outside, try this simple indoor experiment. Walk up and down stairs ten times on the trot. Go on, you can do it. If your grown-ups complain you'll wear out the carpet, smile sweetly and explain – you're climbing the stairs because they are there. You're in good company. That's why one famous climber said he climbed Mount Everest – because it was there! Your grown-ups will be much too mystified to moan.

And that's what this book is all about. Higher than the world's tallest skyscraper, as old as the hills and as icy as the poles, *Freaky Peaks* will have you clinging on for dear life. You can. . .

• scale the dizzy heights of the world's top peaks with Cliff, your trusty mountain guide.

• join the hunt for the hard–to–get yeti (if it exists).

- search for fossil seashells on top of the world (it's true).

- learn how to live through an avalanche (against the odds).

This is geography like never before. And it's horribly gripping. But be warned – don't read this book on your freaky field trip halfway up a mountain. Otherwise, as you're turning the page, you might just fall off the edge. . .

29 May 1953, Mount Everest, Nepal

4 a.m. Dawn was breaking over Mount Everest, the highest place on Earth, bathing the peaks for miles around in a rosy glow. In a tiny, wind-battered tent, precariously perched on a rocky ledge, two men were in the middle of the biggest adventure of their lives.

They were attempting to reach the top of the world, and earn a place in history. Both of them knew they might die trying. No human being had climbed so high before. No one knew if you even could. But it was a risk they were willing to take.

The two men in question were Edmund Hillary and Tenzing Norgay. Back home in New Zealand, Hillary worked in the family bee-keeping business. He'd only been climbing for six short years, though he'd already been to Mount Everest. Norgay was a very experienced Sherpa climber from Nepal, born and raised in the mountains. The year before, he'd climbed to a staggering 8,595 metres up the mountain before fierce winds and freezing cold weather had forced him back. It had been a superhuman effort. But now he was back on Everest, determined to go one better. The two men made a formidable team. Both were tough, brave and fighting fit. Given what lay in store for them, they'd need all these gritty qualities.

They were now in their ninth and final camp, some 8,370 metres up the mountain, having left Camp 8 the day before. Poking their heads anxiously out of the tent door, the men saw that the weather looked fine and settled. For now, at least. The howling wind which had kept them awake most of the night was mercifully still. Even so, the temperature inside their tent had plummeted to an icy –27°C, so bitterly cold that their leather boots had frozen solid. While they had breakfast (tea, lemon juice, biscuits and sardines), Hillary heated the boots slowly over the portable stove to thaw them out.

An hour or so later, after a last, quick check of their oxygen tanks, ropes and ice axes – three crucial pieces of their equipment – they were finally ready to go. At 6.30 a.m., Tenzing and Hillary crawled out of the little tent and set off for their final assault on the summit.

Taking turns to lead, the plucky pair began their long, slow climb towards the South Summit (a peak before the main summit). The first obstacle facing them was a narrow, rocky ridge with sheer drops on either side. Crossing it took great strength and courage. But somehow they made it. No sooner were they safely across than a new hazard loomed. To reach the South Summit, they needed to climb a steep slope of snow. Normally, it was straightforward to cut steps in snow using an ice axe. But here the snow was fine and powdery and covered by an icy crust. It felt like walking on broken eggshells. For every five steps the men climbed, they slid back three as the fragile surface crumbled beneath their feet. Climbing the slippery slope was going to be horribly risky but they knew they could not give up now. They'd come too far for that. Hearts pounding, the two men pressed on and at 9 a.m. they finally reached the South Summit.

Even now, there was no time to relax. Another ridge, sharp as a knife, loomed ahead of them. On one side hung billowing sheets of snow, like massive, icy curtains. Below them lay a sheer drop. On the other side was a huge bank of snow sloping steeply down to a wall of bare, grey rock. It was vital to concentrate now. One false step and they'd surely plummet to their deaths. Roped together for safety, they picked their way gingerly across the snow.

This time, luckily, it was hard and firm and they were able to keep their footing. Step after agonizing step they climbed on, their bodies straining with the effort. A niggling worry lodged in their minds. They had enough oxygen left in their tanks for another four and a half hours. Would that be enough to reach the summit and get back down again? Only time would tell. But without oxygen, they would never make it.

The summit of Everest now looked tantalizingly close. But in the mountains, distances can be deceptive. There were still several hours of hard climbing to go. And now a truly awesome obstacle blocked their path – a vast, vertical step of rock, rising more than 12 metres high, right across the ridge. Their hearts sank. The rock face was so steep and sheer there was simply no way of climbing it. Was this the end? Surely, they'd have to turn back now? Then, to the right of the step, they spotted a narrow crack snaking between the rock and a huge icy overhang (technically called a cornice). This was their only chance. Clinging on for dear life, Hillary wedged himself into the crack and hauled himself up, inch by painstaking inch, using his knees, elbows, shoulders and ice axe. If the ice gave way, as it could anytime, he would plunge to his death on the glacier below.

They were nail-biting minutes. Finally, to Tenzing's great relief, Hillary appeared on a wide ledge at the top of the crack. Now it was Tenzing's turn to follow. So far, so good. But the effort of this nerve-jangling climb had cost the two men dear. For now, they collapsed in exhaustion on the ledge, glad to still be alive. But their minds were made up. They were more determined now than ever before. Whatever else the mountain threw at them, nothing could stop them now.

For two more hours, the men hacked their way upwards, each step a superhuman effort. In the thin mountain air, each breath became harder and harder. It seemed like an endless task. Slowly but surely, their new-found determination began to drain away. Would they ever reach the summit? Then, just above them, they saw a small, snow-covered hump about the size of a haystack. It could have been an icy rock anywhere in the world. Except for one thing – this one was 8,848 metres high. At long, long last, this was the summit of Mount Everest and their journey's end. At 11.30 a.m., on 29 May 1953, five long hours after leaving Camp 9, Edmund Hillary and Tenzing Norgay found themselves standing on top of the world.

Delightedly, the two men shook hands and hugged each other with joy. After all the years of planning and all the failed expeditions, they'd finally made it to the top. There was no need to say anything. Words simply could not express how they both felt. Hillary pulled out his camera and snapped Tenzing waving the flags of Britain, Nepal, India and the United Nations.

Then Tenzing dug a small hole in the snow and buried a pencil, a black cloth cat and some sweets and biscuits, offerings to the mountain gods for guiding them to safety. Alongside them, Hillary buried a crucifix. Then it was time to admire the view. A view no human being had ever seen before – a breathtaking scene of scudding clouds, snow-capped peaks, snaking valleys and glistening glaciers. But their time on the summit could only be short. To save enough oxygen for the descent, they could only stay for 15 minutes. Then it was time for them to go back down to the rest of the expedition, anxiously waiting at the lower camps. Time to come back down to Earth.

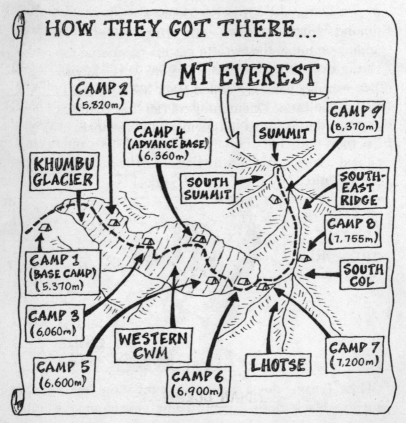

Freaky peak fact file

NAME: Mount Everest
LOCATION: Tibet/Nepal
HEIGHT: 8,848 m
AGE: about 40 million years old
PEAK TYPE: Fold (see page 24)
PEAKY POINTS:

- The highest mountain on Earth.
- It's part of the Himalayas, the highest mountain range.
- It was named after Sir George "Never-rest" Everest (1790-1866), the first person to measure the mountain. He got his nickname for being such a slave-driver. Before this, Mount Everest was boringly called Peak XV.
- It's also called Chomolungma (Mother Goddess of the World) and Sagarmatha (Goddess of the Sky).

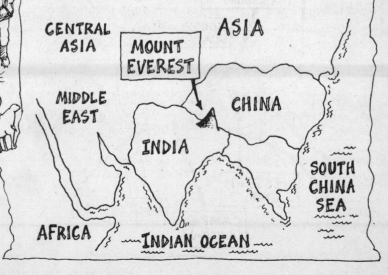

CENTRAL ASIA

ASIA

MOUNT EVEREST

MIDDLE EAST

CHINA

INDIA

SOUTH CHINA SEA

AFRICA

INDIAN OCEAN

So horrible humans had finally gone completely over the top. And Tenzing and Hillary became superstars. They were showered with prizes and top honours (Hillary was made a knight and Tenzing was given the George Medal). Since their record-breaking climb, hundreds of brave (or barmy?) climbers have followed in their footsteps. So if you've got a good head for heights and fancy the adventure of a lifetime, why not face up to a freaky peak of your own? If Everest looks a wee bit scary for starters, don't worry. There are plenty more mountains to climb.

HORRIBLE HEALTH WARNING

Climbing mountains can be horribly dangerous, as you've already seen. So don't go trying it on your own – take a qualified mountaineer with you. Always check the weather before you set out – mountain weather can quickly turn nasty. And always let someone know where you're going and how long you think you're going to be so they can send for help.

MOVING MOUNTAINS

Ask someone to think of a mountain, and they'll most likely describe a boring block of rotten rock, shaped a bit like a pyramid. But there's much more to freaky peaks than that. Honestly! Ask any horrible geographer. (Be warned – geographers love the sound of their own voices. You might be in for a horribly long-winded answer.) They'll tell you freaky peaks cover a fifth of the Earth's surface. That's an awful lot of mountain! But what are freaky peaks and how on Earth did they get there? And why on Earth are they so horribly high? Here's a handy map of some of the highest. . .

What on Earth are freaky peaks?

Strictly speaking, a mountain's a steep-sided rock that rises above the Earth's surface. (Oh, you knew that already?) You measure a mountain by its height above sea level. Even if it's nowhere near the sea. Confusing, eh? Some geographers think proper peaks must be at least 1,000 metres high (that's like three Eiffel Towers plonked on top of each other) if you're going to call them mountains. Others say any old (large-ish) hill or hump will do.

For hundreds of years, mountains had geographers mystified. They knew freaky peaks existed (OK, so you don't have to be a brain surgeon to work that out) but they couldn't agree how they'd got there. Here are some of their over-the-top theories...

According to English vicar Thomas Burnet (1635-1715) the Earth's surface was once as smooth as an eggshell. But God wanted to punish people for their sins. So he cracked the shell open and water poured out. (Remember Noah and the Ark? This is the flood that made them famous.) The slivers of smashed-up shell became mountains. It might sound weird to us now. But astonishingly, a hundred years later, Thomas's eggy theory was still going strong.

Meanwhile, top Scottish geographer James Hutton (1726–1797) had other ground-breaking ideas. He reckoned (rightly) that peaks were pushed up over millions of years by natural forces which twisted and bent the rocks. But he couldn't say what these freaky forces were. James wrote his ideas down in a long, boring book called *Theory of the Earth*. Unfortunately, very few people bothered to read it because his writing was so hard to understand. Besides, they liked the flood story better.

And it didn't stop there. American geologist James Dwight Dana (1813–1895) claimed the Earth was once a red-hot ball of soft, squishy rock. As it cooled, it shrank, and its surface went all dry and wrinkly (like skin on cold school custard. Yuk. Or your fingers in the bath.). The wrinkly bits were freaky peaks. Simple as that.

It seemed that every geographer worth his or her salt had something to say. But, guess what? They still couldn't say

21

exactly how mountains were made. Freaky peaks had them well and truly stumped.

Teacher teaser

Forgotten to do your geography homework? Why not sidetrack your teacher with this painful question:

PLEASE, MISS, DO MOUNTAINS GO TO THE DENTIST?

What on Earth are you talking about?

Answer: No, mountains don't go to the dentist. Lucky things. But your question's not as silly as it seems. You see, British geographer Sir George Airy (1801-1892) reckoned mountains were a bit like teeth. Freaky peaks were the bits you see (like your gleaming, pearly-white gnashers giving a cheesy grin). But underneath they'd got huge, long, rocky roots reaching down into the ground (just like the roots that hold your teeth in your jaw and stop them falling out). Had brilliant but barmy Sir George bitten off more than he could chew? No, he was right.

Earth-moving ideas

But it wasn't until 1910 that geographers finally got to the root of the peaky problem. Then brilliant German geographer Alfred Wegener (1880-1930) had a brainwave. He worked out that the Earth's rocky surface (called the crust – that's the bit of the Earth right beneath your feet) wasn't anything to do with eggshells or custard. Thank goodness for that. Nope. Instead, the rock was cracked into lots of pieces, called plates, a bit like crazy paving (only on a seriously gigantic scale). There were seven huge chunks and lots of smaller ones. But get this: the plates didn't stay put in one place all the time. They were constantly on the move.

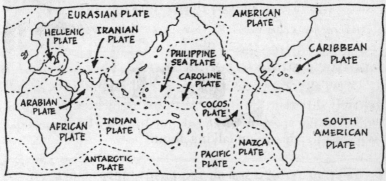

Brainy Alfred called his earth-shattering theory "continental drift". But he couldn't work out what made the plates move. Modern geographers now know the plates float on a layer of hot, gooey rock called magma. It's found underneath the crust (in a layer called the mantle). It's thick and sticky, a bit like treacle. Heat from deep inside the Earth churns up the magma and keeps the crusty plates on their toes.

Normally, the plates drift about without you even noticing. But sometimes, they get in each other's way. Some bash straight into each other. Others try to push and shove their way past. And guess what? Yep, this is how mighty mountains are made. The mystery was over.

Spotter's guide to mountains

It's true, all freaky peaks are rocky and high but they're all horribly different. So if you're thinking of heading for the hills, why not sneak a quick peak in Cliff's useful guidebook. It'll fill you in on the four main types.

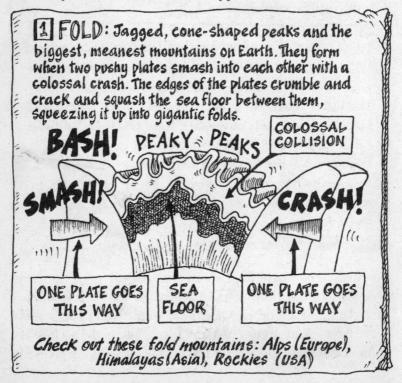

1 FOLD: Jagged, cone-shaped peaks and the biggest, meanest mountains on Earth. They form when two pushy plates smash into each other with a colossal crash. The edges of the plates crumble and crack and squash the sea floor between them, squeezing it up into gigantic folds.

BASH! PEAKY PEAKS COLOSSAL COLLISION

SMASH! CRASH!

ONE PLATE GOES THIS WAY

SEA FLOOR

ONE PLATE GOES THIS WAY

Check out these fold mountains: Alps (Europe), Himalayas (Asia), Rockies (USA)

Are you brave enough to make a freaky fold mountain?

Find out how fold mountains form with this simple but succulent experiment. Then you can eat it for lunch!

What you need:
- four slices of bread
- some marg or butter
- some hard cheese and peanut butter

What you do:

1 Make some nice, thick sandwiches (for the plates of the Earth's crust) with layers of butter, cheese and peanut butter (for the different layers of rocks).

2 Cut the sandwiches in half.

3 Take a sandwich in either hand and squidge them together. (Don't squidge too hard or you'll end up with a soggy mess.)

What happens?

a) your mum tells you off for making a mess

b) the dog steals your sandwiches

c) the sandwiches get squeezed upwards

Answer: c) Congratulations! You've made your own mountains. OK, so you'll need to use your imagination to get the idea. Lucky you didn't have to wait around for the real thing. They take millions and millions of years to form...

ER... I'M MAKING FREAKY PEAKS

YOU'RE THE ONE WHO'S FREAKY

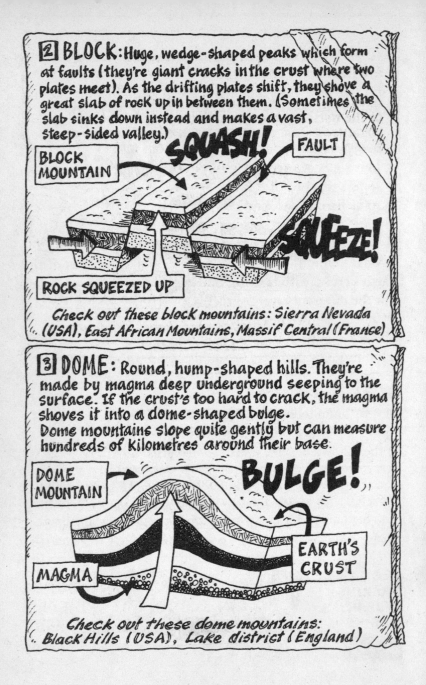

2 BLOCK: Huge, wedge-shaped peaks which form at faults (they're giant cracks in the crust where two plates meet). As the drifting plates shift, they shove a great slab of rock up in between them. (Sometimes the slab sinks down instead and makes a vast, steep-sided valley.)

BLOCK MOUNTAIN

SQUASH!

FAULT

SQUEEZE!

ROCK SQUEEZED UP

Check out these block mountains: Sierra Nevada (USA), East African Mountains, Massif Central (France)

3 DOME: Round, hump-shaped hills. They're made by magma deep underground seeping to the surface. If the crust's too hard to crack, the magma shoves it into a dome-shaped bulge.
Dome mountains slope quite gently but can measure hundreds of kilometres around their base.

DOME MOUNTAIN

BULGE!

EARTH'S CRUST

MAGMA

Check out these dome mountains: Black Hills (USA), Lake district (England)

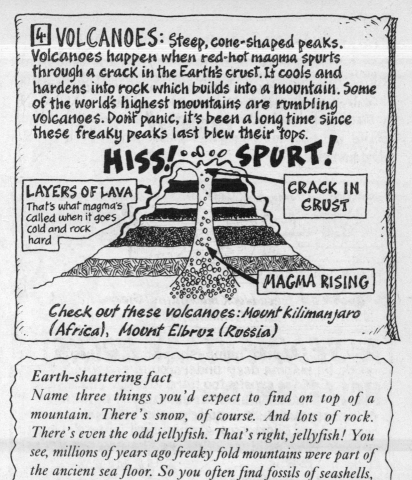

4 VOLCANOES: Steep, cone-shaped peaks.

Volcanoes happen when red-hot magma spurts through a crack in the Earth's crust. It cools and hardens into rock which builds into a mountain. Some of the world's highest mountains are rumbling volcanoes. Don't panic, it's been a long time since these freaky peaks last blew their tops.

HISS! ∘◦O◦∘ SPURT!

LAYERS OF LAVA
That's what magma's called when it goes cold and rock hard

CRACK IN CRUST

MAGMA RISING

Check out these volcanoes: Mount Kilimanjaro (Africa), Mount Elbruz (Russia)

Earth-shattering fact
Name three things you'd expect to find on top of a mountain. There's snow, of course. And lots of rock. There's even the odd jellyfish. That's right, jellyfish! You see, millions of years ago freaky fold mountains were part of the ancient sea floor. So you often find fossils of seashells, jellyfish and other sea animals wedged in the rocks. For years, people thought they'd been stuck there deliberately as a peaky practical joke!

Could you be a geologist?

Ever wondered what on Earth mountains are made from? Rotten rock, of course. Some horrible geographers spend their lives studying rocks. (It's a hard job but someone's got to do it.) The posh name for these rock docs is geologists. Could you be a stony-faced geologist? You'll need a rock-solid knowledge of rocks first.

Getting to know your rock isn't as hard as it sounds. Just remember, all the rocks on Earth belong to one of these three groups. . .

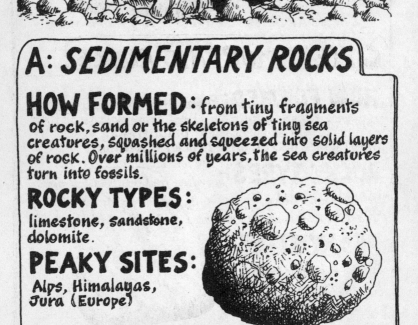

A: SEDIMENTARY ROCKS

HOW FORMED: from tiny fragments of rock, sand or the skeletons of tiny sea creatures, squashed and squeezed into solid layers of rock. Over millions of years, the sea creatures turn into fossils.

ROCKY TYPES: limestone, sandstone, dolomite.

PEAKY SITES: Alps, Himalayas, Jura (Europe)

B: *IGNEOUS ROCKS*

HOW FORMED: from red-hot rocks chucked out of violent volcanoes (that's why they're also called fire rocks), which cool and harden in the air.

ROCKY TYPES:
basalt, andesite, granite.

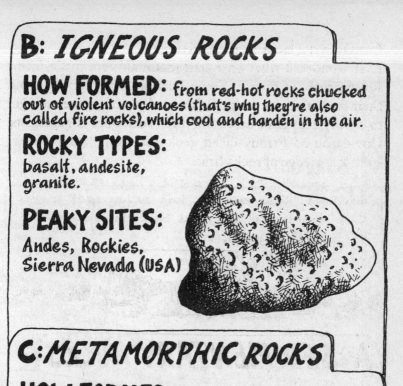

PEAKY SITES:
Andes, Rockies, Sierra Nevada (USA)

C: *METAMORPHIC ROCKS*

HOW FORMED: from sedimentary or igneous rocks cooked by heat from volcanoes or crushed by the forces that build freaky peaks so they change into different rocks altogether.

ROCKY TYPES:
marble, schist, gneiss.

PEAKY SITES:
Alps, Appemines (Italy) Appalachians (USA)

1 BASALT
A SMOOTH, DARK ROCK STUDDED WITH GREEN CRYSTALS. AND THE COMMONEST ROCK ON EARTH.

2 GRANITE
A POLISHED BLEND OF PINKY GREY ROCK AND QUARTZ CRYSTALS. TOUGH BUT TASTY.

3 ANDESITE
SPRINKLED WITH SPECKLES OF BROWN AND GREY. A REAL TASTE OF THE ANDES.(THAT'S HOW IT GETS ITS NAME).

4 LIMESTONE
LAYERS OF LIGHT BROWN AND GREY ROCK, FILLED WITH YUMMY FOSSIL SEA CREATURES.

5 DOLOMITE
GREY AND CRUNCHY WITH A CRYSTAL CENTRE. YOU'LL WANT A WHOLE MOUNTAIN NEXT. (HEAD FOR THE DOLOMITES IN EUROPE IF YOU DO).

6 SANDSTONE
A GRITTY MIXTURE OF SUMPTUOUS SAND GRAINS. MIN(?) IT DOESN'T STICK IN YOUR TEETH.

7 GNEISS (NICE)
TASTY LAYERS OF LIGHT AND(?) ROCK, WITH A CRUNCHY TWIST. GN(?) BY NAME AND NICE BY NATURE.

8 SCHIST
A FLAKY FEAST, THE LITTLE (?) BITS ARE GORGEOUS GARNETS (YOU CAN USE THEM TO MAKE GEOLOGICAL JEWELLERY).

9 MARBLE
PURE WHITE AND CRUMBLY, WIT(?) A TEXTURE LIKE SUGAR, OR HARD (?) STREAKED WITH GREY, PINK OR GR(?) A REALLY CLASSY ROCK CHOC(?)

10 SLATE
GREY AND MADE FROM THE F(?) MUDSTONE. EASY TO CUT INTO SLICE(?)

LOOKING FOR THAT EXTRA-SPECIAL PRESENT ?

FED UP WITH FLOWERS AND SMELLY SOAP ?

Look no further...

FOR THE PERFECT GIFT TO WOW YOUR TEACHER AND IMPRESS YOUR FRIENDS, CHECK OUT A BOX OF OUR NEW, IMPROVED*...

Rotten Rock Chocs

The sweet that'll set your teeth on edge!

GO ON, DIG IN...

* Now with even greater crunchiness!

WARNING! MIND YOUR TEETH WHEN YOU'RE MUNCHING THESE CHOCCIES. THEY'VE GOT HORRIBLY HARD CENTRES.

31

Freaky peak facts

Is your geography teacher at the peak of her powers? Find out with this freaky True/False quiz.

1 Mount Everest is the highest mountain on Earth. TRUE/FALSE?
2 Mount Everest is the tallest mountain on Earth. TRUE/FALSE?
3 The Himalayas are the longest mountain range. TRUE/FALSE?
4 Mountains grow under the sea. TRUE/FALSE?
5 Most mountains are less than 1,000 years old. TRUE/FALSE?
6 There aren't any mountains in Britain. TRUE/FALSE?

Answers:

1 TRUE. At a staggering 8,848 metres high, Everest's officially the highest peak on the planet. It's almost 20 times higher than the world's highest skyscraper. Or as high as your house . . . with another 599 houses on top.

What's more, Everest's still growing. It's true. That's because the two crusty plates that pushed up the Himalayas are still smashing away. Experts reckon Everest's getting about 13 millimetres higher every year. Doesn't sound much, but that makes it more than 50 centimetres higher than it was in Tenzing and Hillary's day.

I THOUGHT WE WERE TRAINING TO CLIMB EVEREST?

WE ARE, WE'VE JUST GOT TO CLIMB MUM'S HOUSE 600 TIMES FIRST

2 FALSE. Everest may be the world's highest peak if you measure it from sea level. But it certainly isn't the tallest. The world-record holder's Mauna Kea in Hawaii. Measured from its bottom, deep under the sea, this vast volcano's an awesome 10,203 metres tall, beating Everest into second place by a massive 1,000 metres (or 1 kilometre) and more. The top half of the mountain pokes out of the sea as a heavenly Hawaiian island. The rest lies hidden underwater.

I DON'T THINK DEEP-SEA MOUNTAIN-CLIMBING IS GOING TO CATCH ON!

3 FALSE. The Andes in South America are over 8,000 kilometres long, making them the longest mountain range on Earth. That's the same distance as from London to Peru (a handy place to start your tour of the Andes from). The awesome Andes snake all the way down the western edge of South America, through seven countries. The Rockies take second place, more than 3,000 kilometres behind.

4 TRUE. There are masses of mountains under the sea. Some stick up to form islands you can see (remember Mauna Kea?). Others aren't high enough to break the surface. A huge range of mountains runs right down the middle of the Atlantic Ocean from Iceland to Antarctica. It's over 11,000 kilometres long (that's like one and a half of the Andes). These peaks pop up when two crusty plates pull apart underwater. Red-hot, runny rock oozes up to plug the gap. It cools and goes solid, and builds freaky peaks.

5 FALSE. Mountains are much, much older than that. Take the ancient Appalchians in the USA. Give or take a few million years, they're at least 400 million years old. Imagine the dinosaurs' surprise when these freaky peaks popped up! In geological time (which is much longer than normal time – is this why your geography lessons seem to last for ever?), the Himalayas are still teenagers. Even though they're about 40 million years old.

HMM, THAT WASN'T THERE YESTERDAY

6 FALSE. If you only count peaks over 1,000 metres high, it's true that England doesn't have any mountains. But in the whole of Britain there are a few. Ben Nevis in Scotland is 1,343 metres high. Pretty puny by freaky peak standards, but still the highest mountain in Britain. People have built a huge cairn (pile of stones) on top which adds another few metres. What d'ya mean, it's cheating?

What your teacher's score means...
If you're feeling generous, award ten points for each correct answer.
50–60 points. Top marks. Your teacher's really reached her peak. Give her a box of Rock Chocs as a prize. (She'll be too

busy picking the bits out of her teeth to give you any homework. You hope.)

30–40 points. Not bad but your teacher's probably peaked to soon. A very up-and-down performance.

20 points and below. Terrible. Your teacher needs to set her sights higher. Much higher. The only way is up from here.

Still trying to pick which peak to head for? Here's a warning. There's no time to lose. You see, mountains won't hang around for ever, however tough they seem. As soon as they're made, they start to wear out. So to find out what's getting the mountains down, cling on by your fingertips to the next cliff-hanging chapter.

FREAKY PEAK   FREAKY PEKE

Freaky peaks look rock-solid but looks can be misleading. It's the same with some geography teachers. They might look nice and kind and reasonable but woe betide you if your homework's late. Then they turn nasty, very nasty indeed.

Mountains take millions of years to form. But no sooner has a peak reared its ugly head than the wind and the weather start wearing it down. You could say it's all downhill from then on (ha! ha!). You can spot a young mountain by its sharp, pointy peaks. As it gets older and wears out, it ends up smooth and round. Horrible geographers call this wearing down erosion. But what on Earth does it mean?

Can you spot the difference?

TABLE MOUNTAIN

MOUNTAINOUS TABLE

Table Mountain's a freaky peak in sunny South Africa. It's been worn into a shape a bit like a table by years of wind and rain. It's even got its own tablecloth (that's the name given to its cover of cloud). Whereas a table's something you eat your tea from and nothing to do with mountains. Obviously.

Erosion – the earth-shattering story

Erosion's the tricky technical term for the way the weather wears peaks away. In time it'll grind them right down into the ground. Freaky or what? Don't worry – you'd need to stick around for millions of years to see this happening. (Though some brand-new peaks might have popped up by then.) Erosion gives freaky peaks their shape. How? On weather-beaten mountains, ice is the main mover and shaker. Here's one way ice wears mountains down. What happens is this. . .

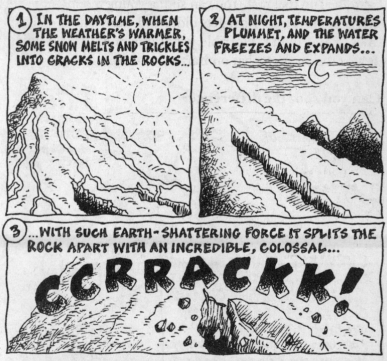

1) IN THE DAYTIME, WHEN THE WEATHER'S WARMER, SOME SNOW MELTS AND TRICKLES INTO CRACKS IN THE ROCKS...

2) AT NIGHT, TEMPERATURES PLUMMET, AND THE WATER FREEZES AND EXPANDS...

3) ...WITH SUCH EARTH-SHATTERING FORCE IT SPLITS THE ROCK APART WITH AN INCREDIBLE, COLOSSAL...

CCRRACKK!

Sometimes seriously huge slabs of ice slip and slide down the mountainside. These are ghastly, grinding glaciers. Are you brave enough to get to know a glacier? Be warned – they're really slippery characters.

What on Earth are glaciers?

1 Glaciers are gigantic rivers of ice found on freaky peaks. But if you can't tear yourself away from the telly, why not get to grips with a slippery glacier from the comfort of your own armchair. Here's Cliff with his stay-at-home glacier guide:

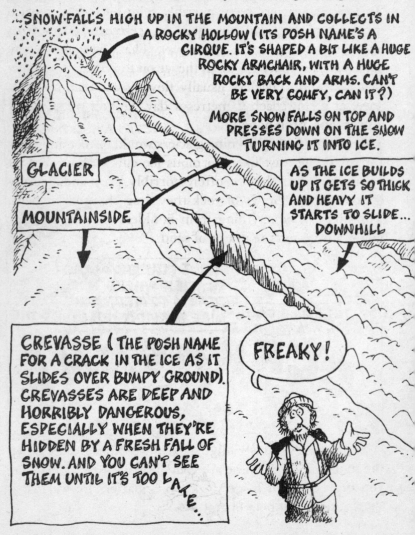

SNOW FALLS HIGH UP IN THE MOUNTAIN AND COLLECTS IN A ROCKY HOLLOW (ITS POSH NAME'S A CIRQUE. IT'S SHAPED A BIT LIKE A HUGE ROCKY ARMCHAIR, WITH A HUGE ROCKY BACK AND ARMS. CAN'T BE VERY COMFY, CAN IT?)

MORE SNOW FALLS ON TOP AND PRESSES DOWN ON THE SNOW TURNING IT INTO ICE.

GLACIER

MOUNTAINSIDE

AS THE ICE BUILDS UP IT GETS SO THICK AND HEAVY IT STARTS TO SLIDE... DOWNHILL

CREVASSE (THE POSH NAME FOR A CRACK IN THE ICE AS IT SLIDES OVER BUMPY GROUND). CREVASSES ARE DEEP AND HORRIBLY DANGEROUS, ESPECIALLY WHEN THEY'RE HIDDEN BY A FRESH FALL OF SNOW. AND YOU CAN'T SEE THEM UNTIL IT'S TOO LATE...

FREAKY!

2 Like rivers, glaciers only flow downhill. Why? What happens is that gravity drags them down. (Gravity is the force which brings things down to the ground. So if you lose your footing on a slippery slope, gravity brings you down to Earth with a bump. Ouch!) But gravity doesn't work alone. To look at, glaciers seem horribly solid but oddly, the ice inside is runny (like those yummy ice-cream lollies with gooey toffee inside . . . delicious). That's because it gets squashed and squeezed by all the ice on top. Then it starts to flow downhill. Glaciers usually flow slower than a snail's pace, at a slowcoach 2 metres a day. So you could easily outrun one. (You hope.)

3 You might think glistening glaciers would be nice and clear and sparkling, just like enormous ice cubes. But you'd be wrong. In fact, they're often horribly grey and grubby because of the tonnes of rock they drag along with them. The bits can be anything from boulders the size of mini mountains to minute grains of sand.

SNOUT (THE END OF THE GLACIER WHERE IT STARTS TO MELT. A BIT LIKE A RUNNY NOSE)

4 Some of the rocky bits get stuck in the ice and give the glacier its cutting edge. As it creeps along, the gritty glacier scratches and scrapes at the mountainside, like a gigantic icy scouring pad, grinding out vast U-shaped valleys. The glacier bulldozes the rest of the rock along in front of it, then dumps it at its snotty snout. The technical term for this pile of rocks is "moraine".

5 Some grinding glaciers are horribly huge. In the high-rise Himalayas, some reach a staggering 70 kilometres long and measure almost a kilometre thick. Imagine having that flowing down your street. But glaciers can shrink as well as grow. This happens when the weather turns warmer and melts the ice at the glacier's snout. Then the glacier starts to shrink in size. The Rhone glacier in the Alps started to melt in 1818. A hundred years later, it had shrunk so much that a hotel famous for its glacier-side view found itself seriously stranded.

6 Boulders aren't the only things you'll find in a ghastly glacier. In 1991, two freaked-out climbers had the shock of their lives. They stumbled across the deep-frozen body of a man poking out of a glacier in the Alps. Gruesome. They found out later that the man had died in a terrible blizzard . . . more than 5,000 years before!

HE LOOKS LIKE MY OLD GEOGRAPHY TEACHER

A tale of two glaciers

Adventurous scientist Louis Agassiz (1807–1873) ended up being so gripped by ice he spent his summer holidays glacier-spotting in Switzerland. (Why not suggest this to your parents?) His sensible family didn't go with him. Most likely they'd already set off for the seaside.

Young Louis lived in Switzerland (so he didn't have far to travel to get to the awesome Alps). As a boy, he was shockingly bright and brainy. When he left school, he went off to university and got not one, but two first-class degrees, in philosophy and medicine. Swotty Louis trained to be a doctor but he gave up medicine to study . . . fish. Yep, fish. Goodness knows what his teachers thought about that. It was all very fishy. But these weren't just any old fish (like the ones you get with a bag of old chips). No. These frightful fish were dead and had been for a very long time. (Imagine the deadly pong. Phwoar!) In fact, they'd been dead for so long they'd turned into fishy fossils.

Later, Louis became professor of natural history at the College of Neuchatel, where he could study his favourite fish to his heart's content. He also wrote several dead boring books, including one all about fossil starfish.

But what on Earth did these freaky fish have to do with glaciers? Nothing at all. You see, Louis got interested in glaciers by accident at a talk given by his old geography teacher. From then on, glaciers had him hooked (now he knew what a fish felt like) and he made some thrilling discoveries. Anyway, here's how he might have reported his finds in his postcards home (if he'd had time to write any).

The Alps, Bex, Switzerland, 1836

Dear Everyone,
                The journey was
fine and I got here safely. It was
good to see old Mr de Charpentier
again. We unpacked our bags then
headed straight for the glaciers.
You remember Mr de C's idea that
glaciers gouge out peaks and
valleys and lug giant rocks
around? (no space, have to send you 2 cards)

Mr & Mrs Agassiz
Cuckoo Gardens
Yodel Way
Switzerland

Postcard 2 ...

Well, I thought he'd lost his
marbles. But he's right. That's
exactly what's happened all
around us. What's more, we've
seen the same features and rocks
in places where it isn't icy. It's a
real puzzle. But Mr de C agrees
with me. There must have been
ancient glaciers there. A very
long time ago. Thanks for the
woolly gloves. Very handy.
          Love from Louis XXX

Mr & Mrs Agassiz
Cuckoo Gardens
Yodel Way
Switzerland

By the way, Mr de Charpentier was
Louis's old teacher. Would you fancy going
on holiday with your geography teacher?

Back home, Louis was invited to talk about glaciers at the
Swiss Society of Natural Sciences. But his ideas met a very
icy reception. One sniffy scientist even told Louis he'd be
better off sticking to fish. But Louis wasn't put off. No way.
He was soon heading off for the hills again. . .

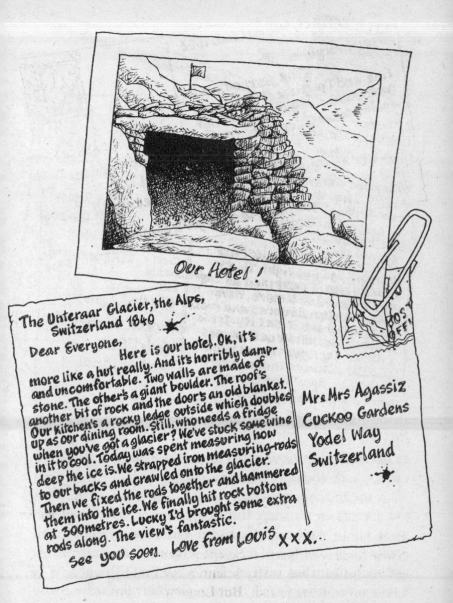

Our Hotel!

The Unteraar Glacier, the Alps,
Switzerland 1840

Dear Everyone,
                Here is our hotel. OK, it's
more like a hut really. And it's horribly damp
and uncomfortable. Two walls are made of
stone. The other's a giant boulder. The roof's
another bit of rock and the door's an old blanket.
Our kitchen's a rocky ledge outside which doubles
up as our dining room. Still, who needs a fridge
when you've got a glacier? We've stuck some wine
in it to cool. Today was spent measuring how
deep the ice is. We strapped iron measuring-rods
to our backs and crawled on to the glacier.
Then we fixed the rods together and hammered
them into the ice. We finally hit rock bottom
at 300 metres. Lucky I'd brought some extra
rods along. The view's fantastic.
        See you soon.   Love from Louis x x x.

Mr & Mrs Agassiz
Cuckoo Gardens
Yodel Way
Switzerland

The Unteraar Glacier, 1841

Dear Everyone,

What a day! Today I decided to explore a crevasse. It seemed easy enough. At first. I was lowered down on a sort of swing. It was brilliant. But I was so busy admiring the colour of the ice (it's a lovely shade of blue, by the way), I didn't notice I'd nearly reached the bottom. I shouted to be pulled up but they didn't hear me clearly. Instead, they lowered me even further down... into an ice-cold pool of water! My feet were freezing. But worse was to come. On the way up, I was almost skewered by ice stalactites, sticking out from the glacier walls. Still it didn't hurt too much. And what an amazing adventure!

Love from Louis X X X

Mr & Mrs Agassiz
Cuckoo Gardens
Yodel Way
Switzerland

Louis's glacier-spotting holidays taught him – and us – a lot about glaciers. About 18,000 years ago, huge slices of ice covered a third of the Earth. In the Alps, the ice was so amazingly thick that only the tips of the highest peaks poked out above it. Today's glistening glaciers are all that were left when the ancient ice melted. Louis's daring discoveries soon put glaciers on the map. But Louis himself gave ice up and went off to America. He never came back. He became professor of zoology at Harvard University and turned his attention to turtles instead. But when he died, aged 66, a boulder was brought all the way from his favourite Swiss glacier to mark his grave.

Freaky peak fact file

NAME: The Alps

LOCATION: Europe (France, Italy, Switzerland, Germany and Austria)

LENGTH: 1,200 km

AGE: about 15 million years old

PEAK TYPE: Fold (see page 24)

PEAKY POINTS:

• They formed when the Eurasian Plate smashed into Africa.

• Mont Blanc in France is the highest peak at 4,807 m.

• Two small streams in the Swiss Alps mark the start of the River Rhine, one of the longest rivers in Europe.

• The longest glacier in the Alps is the Aletsch Glacier in Switzerland. It's 26 km long and the size of a small city.

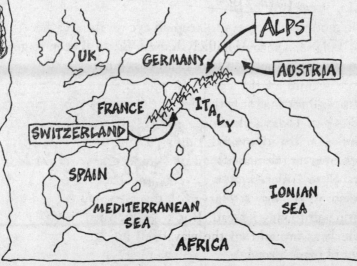

Can you spot the difference?

ROCK·CLIMBING SHEEP	SHEEPISH ROCK

Answer: The posh name for a sheepish rock is a *roche moutonée*. That's French for a sheep-shaped rock. It's the name for a hump of rock gouged out by a glacier. The ice carves out wavy grooves on its surface that look like a sheep's curly wool. (OK, so you'll need to use your imagination for this bit.) It's also the name of a groovy type of wig worn in eighteenth-century France. Must have been a very baaa-d hair day!

Peaky weather report

In the mountains, it pays to keep an eye on the weather. IF YOU WANT TO COME BACK ALIVE. Still keen to go? Then check out Cliff's freaky weather report. . .

Today will start off fine and clear, with clouds gathering in the afternoon. There may be the chance of a blizzard later. Expect howling winds and driving snow higher up. Or it might be calm and sunny. You just never know!

Trouble is, freaky peak weather is horribly fickle and unpredictable. One minute, it's nice and warm and sunny, the next it's blowing up a storm. Here are four types of weather a mountain might fling at you . . . IN AN HOUR.

Freezing cold. You might think the higher up you go, the warmer the weather gets. After all, you're closer to the sun. But you'd be wrong. Dead wrong. For every 100 metres you climb, it gets about 1°C colder. This is because the air high up is thin and clear. It doesn't contain any dusty specks that trap and give out heat from the sun. At the top of Mount Everest, temperatures can plummet as low as –60°C. That's as cold as the coldest day you can possibly imagine, only ten times worse. Plenty cold enough to freeze you to death.

HELLO BASECAMP, CAN YOU SEND ME UP ANOTHER 20 PAIRS OF SOCKS? OVER.

Even in summer, it's well below freezing. That's why some perishing peaks are permanently capped with snow, even if they're in warm places. Like Mount Kilimanjaro in Africa – its freaky peak is covered in glaciers all year round even though it's only a few kilometres south of the steamy equator.

Chilly winds. Wind's a real problem up in the mountains. (No, not *that* sort of wind.) By day, the wind blows up the mountainside. At night, it blows the other way. In a matter of minutes, a gale can be gusting along at a speedy 130 kilometres per hour, as fast as a fast car. Fast enough to knock you right off your feet. Or blow you off the mountainside.

What's worse, the wind makes it feel even chillier than it actually is. If the wind's blowing at 50 km/h and the temperature's –35°C, you'd freeze solid in 30 seconds. Brrr! So wrap up warm.

Lethal lightning. Lightning always takes the quickest path to the ground and hits the nearest target. So watch out if you're standing on a hill-top admiring the view: that could be you! You might end up being fried to a crisp. Or battered and bruised by rock-hard hail that falls in thunderstorms. Watch out for puffy, cauliflower-shaped clouds. They're a tell-tale sign there's a storm on the way. Or you might feel your hair standing on end (that's because of electricity in the air). Freaky. Crouch down low, until the storm blows over.

Blinding blizzards. Blizzards are horribly savage snow storms and they can strike without warning. You'll know when a blizzard hits – temperatures plummet and howling winds blast the snow straight into your mouth . . . so you can hardly breathe. Most of the time you can't see anything either. Blizzards can have tragic results. In fact, more climbers die from being battered by blizzards than by falling.

HORRIBLE HEALTH WARNING!

If you climb a mountain near sunrise or sunset, don't look behind you. You might see a huge, shadowy figure one step behind. Have you seen a ghost? Aaagghh! DON'T PANIC! The freaky fiend is your own shadow. Honestly. It's called the spectre of the Brocken after the Brocken Mountain in Germany where it's often seen. And there's a horribly straightforward reason for it. At sunrise and sunset, the sun is low in the sky and casts your shadow on nearby clouds. Only much, much bigger than usual. And you see a ghastly, ghostly figure. Phew!

One thing's for certain. Wind, snow or shine, it's tough at the top. Horribly tough and hostile. But apart from sinister shadows and sheepish rocks, surely nothing on Earth would want to live there. Would it? Oh yes, it would. Get ready for a high-rise surprise. . .

FREAKY NATURE

You won't find anything living right at the tops of the highest peaks. It's just too bloomin' windy and cold. But take a peek further downhill and you'll meet some horribly hardy wildlife. Peaks are perilous places to live. But, oddly enough, some plants and animals find the freezing temperatures rather bracing. They happily cope with the slippery slopes and the stormy weather. So how on Earth do they do it? The first thing to find out is which bit of the freaky peak these tough nuts call home.

WE MAY LOOK CUTE AND FLUFFY BUT IT TAKES GUTS TO SURVIVE UP HERE, YOU KNOW

Life at the top

Test your teacher's nature know-how with this tricky question: Where do you find steamy rainforests, bone-dry deserts and icy poles . . . all in one place? Does he or she give up? Now show off by giving the answer – it's on a freaky peak, of course. As you go uphill, the weather changes (it gets colder the higher you go, remember?). So you start off sweltering at the bottom but break out in goose pimples near the top. Brrrr! This gives lots of different habitats (that's the posh scientific word for plant and animal homes).

Time to make friends with some freaky wildlife. Or, if you don't want to end up as a mountain lion's lunch, you could always send Cliff instead. . .

51

TAHR (MOUNTAIN GOAT)

BLACK BEAR

PIKA

SNOWCOCK

LANGUR

TIGER

YOU START HERE

TREE LINE

AN IMAGINARY LINE HIGH UP ON THE MOUNTAIN. IT'S THE HIGHEST PLACE YOU'LL FIND TREES. ABOVE THIS, IT'S TOO COLD AND WINDY FOR THEM TO GROW

CONIFEROUS TREES

CONIFERS ARE TREES LIKE PINES, FIRS AND SPRUCES (AND CHRISTMAS TREES). MIND YOUR HEAD IF YOU'RE UNDERNEATH ONE. THEY'RE A BRILLIANT SHAPE FOR SHRUGGING OFF SNOW. IT SIMPLY SLIDES OFF THEIR SLANTING BRANCHES. CRASHH!

DECIDUOUS FOREST

YOU START YOUR CLIMB IN A WARM FOREST OF SHADY OAK AND TEAK TREES (DECIDUOUS MEANS THEY LOSE THEIR LEAVES). ON OTHER PEAKS, YOU'LL FIND GRASSY PLAINS OR STEAMY RAINFOREST INSTEAD. WATCH OUT FOR HUNGRY BEARS...

Freaky peak fact file

NAME: Himalayas

LOCATION: Asia (India, Nepal, Bhutan, Pakistan, China/Tibet, Afghanistan)

LENGTH: about 2,600 km

AGE: 30-50 million years old

PEAK TYPE: Fold (see page 24)

PEAKY POINTS:

• Their name means "abode of snow" in the ancient Indian language.

• They're the world's highest mountains with nine of the world's top ten peaks. Mount Everest's the highest.

• They're carved into shape by huge glaciers and chunks of ice.

• In the Hindu and Buddhist religions, they're believed to be the homes of the gods.

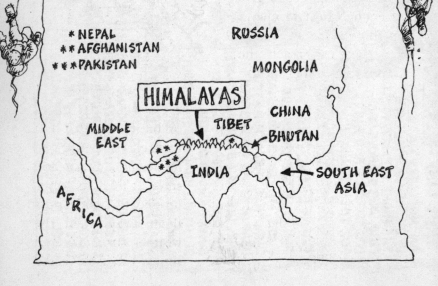

* NEPAL
** AFGHANISTAN
*** PAKISTAN

RUSSIA

MONGOLIA

HIMALAYAS

TIBET

CHINA

BHUTAN

MIDDLE EAST

INDIA

SOUTH EAST ASIA

AFRICA

Peaky plant survival

You might think that faced with the cold, the wind and the dry, rocky soil, peaky plants might curl up and die. After all, without water and warmth, their cells would freeze solid and they couldn't make any food. Pretty disastrous, eh? But plenty of plucky plants grow on peaks. It's a bloomin' miracle how they do it. Luckily, they've got lots of sneaky tricks up their sleeves (sorry, leaves) to help them survive. Which of these life-saving strategies are too strange to be true?

1 The tiny shoots of the Alpine snowbell look fine and delicate. But if you picked a bunch of these for your mum, you might end up getting your fingers burned. These little beauties can give off enough heat to melt a hole in the snow. That's how they can reach the surface to bloom in spring. TRUE/FALSE?

OOH! OWW! OOH! ARGH!

2 The Rocky Mountain umbrella plant has umbrella-shaped leaves for keeping off rain and snow. It folds its leaves up neatly and puts them away when the weather turns dry and sunny. TRUE/FALSE?

3 The saussurea plant from the Himalayas is a type of daisy. But you wouldn't want to try making daisy chains with it. Its leaves are so furry and warm that bees love to snuggle up in them. And they don't like being disturbed. TRUE/FALSE?

4 Lichens grow slowly. Horribly slowly. A patch the size of a school dinner plate may be thousands of years old. This is because there may only be one day every year when it's warm enough to grow. These plants are ideal for peaks because they can eat rock. They make acids which dissolve the rocks and make them crumble. Then they send out tiny "roots" to suck up goodness from the rocks. TRUE/FALSE?

5 Some mountain trees, like willow trees, grow only a few centimetres tall. In fact, they're so small you can step right over them. They grow so low to keep out of the howling wind. Some people call them "elfin wood" because you'd have to be as titchy as an elf to count them as a wood. TRUE/FALSE?

Answers: They're all TRUE except for 2. You do get umbrella plants but not on mountains and they can't put their umbrellas up and down.

Earth-shattering fact

Most peaky plants grow close to the ground to keep out of the wind. But not all. . . Some peculiar plants called lobelias and groundsels grow on the slopes of Mount Kenya in Africa. These giants can shoot up to 10 metres tall. (That's like five geography teachers standing on each other's shoulders.) But nobody knows why. In other places, they're horribly puny and small. By the way, giant groundsels are related to weedy dandelions. Imagine a dandelion that tall growing in your garden!

THESE DANDELIONS HAVE GOT TO GO

Freaky creature lifestyles

You might not think so but you have life easy. If you're cold, you just have to put on a jumper. If you're peckish, well, just raid the fridge. See? Easy, peasy. Compared to a mountain creature, at least – they have things horribly tough. But freaky creatures are fighting back. They've developed lots of cunning ways of coping with the weather and the slippery slopes (without freezing to death or falling off). Can you match each of the mountain creatures on page 58 to its horrible high-rise lifestyle?

1 Its dark brown colouring helps keep it warm (dark colours are better than paler colours for soaking up the sun). It lives high up on Mount Everest and eats tiny grains of pollen blown up by the wind.

2 Its thick woolly coat's so toasty warm, it sometimes gets too hot. But it also has bare patches on its legs. To cool down, it sticks its bum in the air, facing the wind. Its other horrible habit is spitting bits of smelly, chewed-up food at its enemies. (DON'T try either of these things at home.) Its cousin's a camel and it lives in the Andes.

3 It lives in the mountains of northern Japan and keeps warm in winter by taking a long, hot bath in a volcanic spring. Outside the temperature's a chilly –15°C. In the water, it's a steaming 43°C. It always tests the water first so it doesn't get its toes toasted.

4 Its hooves have sharp

A MACAQUE

B MOUNTAIN GOAT

C SPINY LIZARD

58

edges which dig into cracks in the rocks and are hollow for sticking on to rocks, like squishy suction pads. It's brilliant at climbing and can walk along the narrowest ledges without falling off.

5 It picks up a bone from a dead goat or sheep and flies to the top of a freaky peak. Then it drops the bone on the rocks below to smash it open. It swoops down and picks at the bits of bone, especially the juicy middle.

6 It lives high on the slopes of a vile volcano in Mexico. It can cope with being frozen solid for a whole day and night, then it thaws out in the sun.

Ⓓ VICUNA

Ⓔ GLACIER FLEA

Ⓕ LAMMERGEIER

Answers: 1 e); 2 d); 3 a); 4 b); 5 f); 6 c)

Way past your bedtime

Some peaky creatures find the best way to stay warm is by sleeping through winter and not waking up until spring. This is called hibernation. It's a good idea on a freaky peak because animals need loads of food to keep warm in cold weather. But in winter there's not much food around. So where better to be than snugly tucked up in bed? Finding it hard to stay awake? Why not spend a year with an alpine marmot?

A year in the life of an alpine marmot

Summer

You spend summer stuffing your face with food ready for the winter. Your favourite nibbles are seeds, buds and mushrooms. But you're so hungry any old mountain plants will do. You eat so much and get so fat it's a tight squeeze getting through the door of your burrow.

MUNCH!
MUNCH!
MUNCH!

Autumn

You line your burrow with cosy grass and get ready for a good long kip. Actually, it's a bit of a squash - the whole family sleeps huddled close together. So you might have 14 other marmots snoring away, right in your ear. (One little sister's bad enough. . .) The last one in plugs up the entrance with some hay, earth and stones. You curl up into a ball and then it's off to sleep. Zzzzzz.

MOVE OVER   GET OFF!

Winter

Outside the weather's freezing cold but you're much too sleepy and snug to care. You don't even notice your breathing and pulse rates have slowed right down and your body temperature has dropped. You don't feel hungry because you live off all that extra body fat you built up in the summer. Every three to four weeks you wake up to have a poo and a wee. Good job you're too tired to notice the pong.

Spring

Wakey, wakey! Rise and shine. You've been fast asleep for SIX WHOLE MONTHS. What d'ya mean you're still sleepy? You've lost about a quarter of your body weight - say hello to the new, slim-line you! Now it's time to go out into the big, wide world . . . and to spring clean your smelly burrow!

A freaky mountain mystery

Many peaky creatures are horribly shy. It's hard enough just staying alive without making friends as well. But there's one animal that's more mysterious than most. In fact, it's a mystery if it exists at all. What on Earth could this freaky beast be? Brace yourself. You're about to find out. . .

For centuries, people in the Himalayas have told stories of a huge, shaggy-haired creature called a yeti roaming the mountains. Is it a man? Is it an ape? Nobody knows. You see, no one has ever got close enough to a yeti to find out for sure. And there aren't any yetis in wildlife parks or zoos for horrible scientists to study. So we decided to send our own expedition to track down a real-live yeti. Plenty of other expeditions had tried and failed. Would we be the first to come face-to-face with this elusive beast? But first we needed a volunteer. Someone incredibly brave and intrepid. Someone who didn't feel the cold. Someone just like Cliff, the climber. . .

IF YOU'RE AFTER SOMEONE BRAVE AND... **WHAT WAS THAT?**

Here's Cliff's report and it makes riveting reading. Go on, take a peek . . . if you dare.

The Case of the Missing YETI

You know me, I love a good mountain. That's why I took this job. It seemed right up my street (or should that be peak, ha! ha!). Besides, I'd seen these detective dudes on the telly and it looked like a cinch. That was my first big mistake. Anyway, my first job was to interview the suspect. It was easier said than done. I decided to hit the top secret files and find out exactly what I was up against.

1 The suspect

NAME: Yeti
DESCRIPTION:

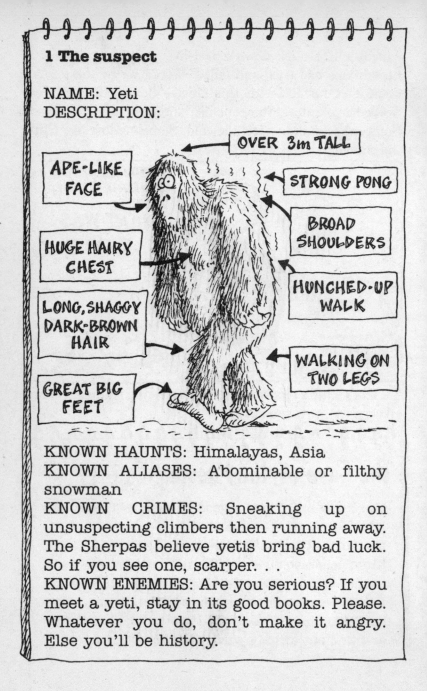

OVER 3m TALL

APE-LIKE FACE

STRONG PONG

BROAD SHOULDERS

HUGE HAIRY CHEST

HUNCHED-UP WALK

LONG, SHAGGY DARK-BROWN HAIR

WALKING ON TWO LEGS

GREAT BIG FEET

KNOWN HAUNTS: Himalayas, Asia

KNOWN ALIASES: Abominable or filthy snowman

KNOWN CRIMES: Sneaking up on unsuspecting climbers then running away. The Sherpas believe yetis bring bad luck. So if you see one, scarper. . .

KNOWN ENEMIES: Are you serious? If you meet a yeti, stay in its good books. Please. Whatever you do, don't make it angry. Else you'll be history.

NOTE: Get this. Similar creatures have been seen in the Rockies where they go by the name of Bigfoot or Sasquatch. You also get these freaky beasts in China, Australia, Russia and Africa. Is nowhere safe?

Bigfoot

Me

2 Video diary from the scene of the crime

Cunningly disguised as a, er, yeti, I headed for the Himalayas to investigate the scene of the crime. First stop was Mount Annapurna where several yetis have been spotted in recent years. One was seen (and heard) by two British climbers as they were setting up their camp. They watched it wander about for ten minutes or so before it vanished. Apparently.

10:22

REC●

Well, things have started off well, I must say. I'd only been here for a few hours when I stumbled across a steaming pile of dung. Actually I put my foot straight in it. I've taken a sample to study later (the things we geographers have to do) but I'm pretty certain it's yeti poo. And on one of my late night walks (more later), I spotted some footprints in the snow. They're not mine and there's no one else around. Very suspicious. So who on Earth do they belong to?

13:15

RECO

A few days later. . .

The trail's gone cold. I've been here for over a week now and I still haven't seen an actual yeti in the flesh. Trouble is, yetis are said to be nocturnal (they only come out at night). So they're horribly hard to see in the dark.

09:32

RECO

A few more days later. . .

> What's more, someone or something's pinched the last of the sausages I was saving for my tea. One thing's for sure, there aren't any yetis in this neck of the woods. I'm outta here.

15:59   BAT LOW   REC

3 The evidence

So far, my mission hadn't been a great success. I was the first to admit it. There was only one thing to do – I decided to head home and hit the files again. (Goodbye, yeti suit. Hoorah!) It was time to get to grips with the evidence. Fortunately, other yeti hunters have been luckier than me. So what had they found out so far?

1 Eyewitness accounts. There have been hundreds of sightings of a yeti. And several serious scientific expeditions have set off to catch one and bring it back. In the 1980s, a Canadian climber, Robert Hutchinson, launched Yeti '88, the most ambitious yeti hunt ever.

He wanted to find a yeti and collect some yeti poo (smelly but brilliant scientific evidence, as I found out). He spent five months following yeti tracks but sadly the yeti

that made them kept giving him the slip. I know just how he felt.

2 Frozen footprints. In 1951, top British explorer, Eric Shipton, snapped a trail of giant footprints high up on Mount Everest. Each foot had three small toes and

one much bigger toe. No human could have made them. The only creature the feet might fit was an orang utan (but orang utans live thousands of kilometres away) . . . or a yeti.

3 Sacred scalps. One expedition claimed to have seen an actual scalp from a yeti. It was long and cone-shaped and covered in short, reddish hair. It was kept in a Buddhist monastery near Mount Everest. The monks worshipped the scalp as a sacred relic (that's a precious holy object). The scalp was taken back to London and examined under a

microscope. Sadly, the scientists said it wasn't a yeti's but belonged to a boring mountain goat. But even scientists can be wrong sometimes, can't they?

4 The verdict

So the evidence was mounting up. But what would the final verdict be? Did yetis exist? Or was the whole thing a load of old yeti poo? Anyway, I'd done my bit. I'd even kind of enjoyed it. But now it was time to hand the whole freaky case over to the experts. . .

No, yetis don't exist. Don't be silly. The photos and footprints must be fakes. All you need is a pair of yeti-print boots and the rest is easy. Besides, the thin mountain air plays terrible tricks on you. You might think you've seen something spooky but it's all in the mind. But if there is something there, and I only say maybe, my guess is it's a bear or a (large-ish) monkey. (Which also explains all that poo.)

YETI?
SPAGHETTI

Of course yetis exist. Everyone knows that. OK so scientists haven't caught one yet but it's just a matter of time. They're either a brand-new giant ape yeti, sorry, yet, to be discovered by science. Or a descendant of ancient horrible humans who've been hiding in the mountains for years and years. Who knows, it could be a long-lost relation?

You might think yetis are about as freaky and far out as it gets. But you'd be wrong. Horribly wrong. There are some far stranger creatures lurking on the mountainside. The question is, are you brave enough to meet them? Turn the page quietly in case you disturb them. . .

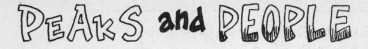

PEAKS and PEOPLE

If you were looking for somewhere to live, what would it be like? Hot and sunny? Near the sea? Nowhere near a freaky peak? Surely no one would want to live there? Well, you're wrong. Despite the horribly harsh conditions, an amazing 500 million people – that's about a tenth of the world's population – live on mountains. So how on Earth do these peaky people cope with their high-rise lifestyle?

Peaky people

The Quechua Indians live high up in the Andes mountains in South America. They mostly live by farming crops, such as potatoes, barley and maize. They also keep cattle, sheep, chickens and . . . llamas. If you're going to live on a mountain, a llama's a horribly useful animal to have. They're brilliant for riding and carrying heavy loads, and you can weave their super-soft wool into toasty warm clothes. By the way, llamas are close cousins of camels, except they don't have humps.

But if you're thinking of paying a Quechua village a visit, be warned. As you go higher, the thin mountain air might leave you feeling dizzy and gasping for breath. That's why the hardy Quechua have slightly bigger hearts and lungs than most people to carry more oxygen in their blood.

They've also found ways of coping with the freezing mountain temperatures: while you're pulling on another pair of thick, llama-wool socks, they'll happily walk barefoot in the snow. That's because their feet have extra blood vessels which stop them getting cold, so they're less likely to get frostbite. An amazing feet, sorry, feat.

Freaky peak fact file

NAME: The Andes

LOCATION: South America (Argentina, Chile, Bolivia, Peru, Ecuador, Columbia, Venezuela)

LENGTH: 7,250 km

AGE: 138-165 million years old

PEAK TYPE: Fold (see page 24)

PEAKY POINTS:

- They're the longest mountain range in the world
- Their highest peak is Aconcagua (6,960 m). This freaky peak's name means "Guard of Stone".
- They formed when the Pacific Ocean plate plunged under South America.
- They're so high they block winds and rain clouds. So it rains on the east side but on the west lies dusty desert.

Peaky perks

Living in the mountains is horribly hard and many peaky people are very poor and struggle to survive. That's why many are now leaving the mountains behind to try their luck in big towns and cities.

But it isn't all doom and gloom. Even the freakiest peaks have their uses. Here are four freaky things you might not expect to find up a perilous peak:

1 Wonderful water. Forget banana milkshakes or cans of fizzy pop, if you're thirsty you can't beat a glass of water. In fact, wonderful water's vital for keeping you alive. Without it, you'd be dead in days. Most of our drinking water comes from raging rivers. But do you know where these rivers start? Up freaky peaks, of course. Some of the biggest rivers on Earth start off as bubbling mountain streams. Some leak from lofty hillside lakes. Others glug from the ends of icy glaciers.

Believe it or not, about half of all the world's drinking water comes from these freaky flows.

2 Shocking electricity. But water's not just for drinking. You can also make electricity from it. (Think about that next time you switch on your computer.) If you live near a mountain, here's what might be happening. . .

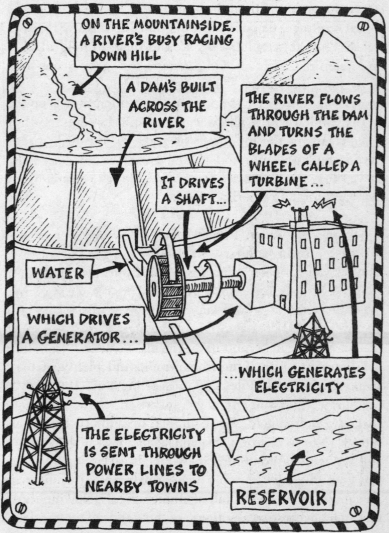

ON THE MOUNTAINSIDE, A RIVER'S BUSY RACING DOWN HILL

A DAM'S BUILT ACROSS THE RIVER

THE RIVER FLOWS THROUGH THE DAM AND TURNS THE BLADES OF A WHEEL CALLED A TURBINE...

IT DRIVES A SHAFT...

WATER

WHICH DRIVES A GENERATOR...

...WHICH GENERATES ELECTRICITY

THE ELECTRICITY IS SENT THROUGH POWER LINES TO NEARBY TOWNS

RESERVOIR

3 Fragile fields. Many peaky people make their living by farming. But it's a horribly hard and back-breaking job. You won't find a nice, flat green field to plant crops in. The soil's much too poor and dusty, and the slope's too slippery and steep. So what on Earth do farmers do? Sherpa farmers in Nepal cut huge, flat steps into the hillside and use them as fields. Then they build walls around them to hold the soil and water in. Clever, eh? On the steps, they grow crops such as potatoes, rice, wheat, barley and apricots. They also keep animals like sheep, goats and cattle. In winter, they keep the animals indoors or in the warmer valleys. In summer, they drive them up the mountain to graze on the lush, green pasture high up.

4 Glittering gold. One thing you'll find plenty of up a freaky peak is rock. Piles and piles of the stuff. But scratch the surface and you might be surprised. Some mountain rocks are rich in gold, silver, copper, tin and other precious metals. (Not to mention gorgeous gemstones such as rubies and emeralds.) And mining these metals is very big business. But gold-digging's horribly dicey. You might strike lucky or you might not. And it takes time to dig a gold mine in a mountain because some mines are thousands of metres deep.

But if you're fed up with paltry pocket money, why not get rich quick and go panning for gold?

What you need:
- a large sieve or pan
- a mountain stream
- a touchstone (a dark rock)
- bags of patience

What you do:

a) Dip your sieve into the stream and fill it with sand and water.

b) Carefully swirl your sieve round to swill the sand and water away.

c) Any gold will settle in the bottom of your sieve as flakes, grains or nuggets.

d) To see if your gold's real, scratch it with your touchstone. If it leaves a yellow streak . . . congratulations! You've struck lucky. (If it doesn't, more fool you. It's probably a rock called pyrite or "fool's gold".)

Freaky peak transport

OK, so your arms ache from all that sieving but at least you're filthy rich. The question is, what on Earth are you going to spend your gold on? If you're living on a far-out peak, you can't just pop along to the shops. They're most likely miles and miles away. (On the bright side, this could make getting to school pretty tricky. Hoorah!) So how do peaky people get from A to B? If you're planning a freaky journey, check out the timetable below. You don't want to miss the bus, do you? There may not be another one along for weeks and weeks. Here's Cliff to see you off.

PEAKY TRANSPORT TIMETABLE

1 Walking tours

Feeling fit? Put your best foot forward and walk. That's how most peaky people get about. The Sherpa people are so super-fit and hardy, they're hired to lug climbers' bags up the mountainside. (Talk about cheating!) The Sherpas live high up in the Himalayas in Nepal, especially around Mount Everest. They can walk for hours and hours, using an even, padding stride that's very energy-efficient. And the Sherpas know all the best places to stop for a rest. By the way, they believe that the peaks are home to the mountain gods. So they always say a prayer or two for a safe journey before setting off.

I WONDER IF HE COULD CARRY ME AS WELL!

- Journey time: Depends how fast you walk.
- Risk of breakdown: Depends how fit you're feeling.

HORRIBLE HEALTH WARNING

Never mess with mountain gods. They've got really terrible tempers. A legend tells of a greedy chief who sent his army up Mount Kilimanjaro to collect the shimmering silver on top. (OK, so you know it's a glacier but he'd never even heard of such a thing.) Only one warrior lived to tell the freaky tale. He said the gods killed the men, and made their fingers and toes drop off (he hadn't heard of frostbite either). As for the silver? Well, it turned to water in their hands. Of course.

2 Yak-back riding

Hitch a lift on a yak for hikes above 6,000 metres. With their long, shaggy coats, these freaky creatures don't feel the cold. And they'll take the steepest slopes and fastest rivers in their stride. A serious expedition up Everest uses 60 yaks to carry its gear. What's more, you can use yak's milk for making butter and yoghurt, the hide for boots, and the hair for handy ropes. You can even eat yaks, if you're desperate. Expecting a letter? Watch out for the yak-back post.

I SEEM TO BE YAK-TO-FRONT!

- Journey time: Yak pace is about the same as walking pace, even with you on its back.
- Risk of breakdown: Very low. Yaks are terrifically tough. But if your yak plays up, try pinching its nose with your thumb and middle finger. Then hold on tight!

3 Take the tunnel

For an easy ride, head for a tunnel. They carry roads and railways through mountainsides. (Otherwise you'd just have to go the long way round!) There are plenty of tunnels around the world, especially in the Alps. The first one ever was the Mont Cenis tunnel between Italy and France built in 1857. It was 13 kilometres long. First, the tunnellers had to blast their way through the solid rock using tonnes of dynamite. Then they dug and drilled out the loose rock. It was stuffy, airless and the rocks got horribly hot. No wonder the tunnel took 13 long years to finish.

I'LL BE GLAD TO SEE THE LIGHT AT THE END OF THIS TUNNEL

- Journey time: About five minutes to drive straight through the Mont Cenis tunnel to get from Italy to France.
- Risk of breakdown: Quite low. Today's tunnels are massively strong but there's still a risk of fatal fires.

4 Hit the high road

If you get car-sick on the way to school, you might like to skip the next bit. Building a road up a mountainside is an amazing engineering feat. You can't just build a nice straight road up and down — the slope's too steep for that. So engineers have to build extra-long, extra-twisty roads with loads of horribly scary "hairpin" bends. (They're called hairpins because they look like those wiggly wire things that keep your granny's hair in place.) Talk about going round the bend. Where's that sick bag. . .?

THIS IS DRIVING ME ROUND THE BEND!

- Journey time: Take it slowly. Very slowly. And watch out for rockfalls and avalanches.
- Risk of breakdown: Check your brakes before you set out. And don't get too close to the edge.

5 Go by train

Let the train take the strain. But get ready for a rocky ride. Like roads, railways can't go straight up and down. They have to snake up slopes in giant loops and zig-zags. On very steep slopes, an extra wheel on the train fits into an extra bit of track to stop the train slipping backwards. If you're feeling brave, hop on the Trans-Andean mountain railway in Chile. In places, the train chugs along at over 4,500 metres. It'll take your breath away. Passengers are given oxygen to stop them feeling queasy in the thin mountain air. Don't forget to pack a picnic and wrap up warm – there's no food or heating on board.

- Journey time: The journey on the Trans-Andean should take about 30 hours but allow a couple of days. It never leaves or arrives on time.
- Risk of breakdown: Quite high. Add another day on to your journey time.

And finally. . .

While you're recovering from your hair-raising journey, here's some good news: freaky peak living is good for your health. It's official. In the Caucasus Mountains, people regularly live to 100 years old. Even your geography teacher isn't that ancient. They put it down to the bracing mountain air and . . . yoghurt. Yes, yoghurt. A good, big bowlful every day. So stock up the fridge and get slurping. . .

CLIMB EVERY MOUNTAIN

Each year, thousands of horribly hardy humans climb up freaky peaks. FOR FUN! If you ask them why, they'll probably look rather sheepish and mutter about good exercise and the stunning views. Or they'll say it's because the mountains are there (remember the stair experiment?). A barmy but brilliant excuse. Why not try it next time your mum catches you scoffing the last of the choccy chip ice-cream? So are these crazy climbers mad, bad or hopelessly lost? Read on and find out. You'll be gripped*.

* Apart from meaning horribly excited, "gripped" is also a term climbers use. It means being so scared stiff you can't move a single muscle. You can't climb up. You can't climb down. You can only cling on for dear life. Don't say you weren't warned. . .

Reaching for the top

Impress your teacher and freak out your friends with some fascinating facts about mad mountaineers. That way you can climb every mountain without leaving your armchair.

The first person known to climb a mountain simply for the thrill of getting to the top was dashing French captain, Antoine de Ville. In June 1492, King Charles VIII ordered him to lead a group of climbers to the top of Mont Aiguille, a 2,097-metre peak in the Alps. (Mont Aguille's French for Needle

Mountain. No wonder when you see its nasty needle-sharp peak. Ouch!) In those days it paid to keep the king happy. Otherwise it might be your head on the chopping block. Anyway, daring de Ville clambered up Needle Mountain on a series of ladders and was so impressed by the stunning views, he stayed on the summit for three whole days. (He also thought it made him look ever so important. What a show-off!)

But climbing mountains for fun was horribly slow to catch on. Local people especially kept freaky peaks at arm's length. The further away, the better. They thought they were full of witches and demons. They might climb a mountain to get from A to B. But sightseeing was out. It wasn't until 1760, almost 300 years after Antoine's lofty ascent, that anyone took mountain climbing seriously. Then top Swiss geographer, Horace Bénédict de Saussure, offered a cash prize to the first person to climb mighty Mont Blanc, the highest peak in Europe. Even then, it took 26 long years for a willing victim, sorry, volunteer to come forward. . .

Melting moments on Mont Blanc

Dr Michel-Gabriel Paccard from Chamonix, France, had spent years gawping at Mont Blanc through his telescope. That freaky peak had him hooked. He tried to climb it a couple of times but couldn't quite reach the top. But he wasn't about to give up now. Oh, no. Besides, Horace's dosh would come in handy. So, at 4.30 a.m. on 8 August 1786, plucky Dr Paccard set off. With him, he took Jacques Balmat, a local crystal hunter, who knew the mountain like the back of his hand. (Except for the very top bit, of course.) As for climbing kit? Well, between them, they had a walking stick each, some bread, meat and a threadbare blanket. Woe betide them if a blizzard struck.

From the start, the going was horribly hard. The trouble was, the weather was warm for the time of year and the ice kept melting beneath them. The only way to cross the colossal crevasses was to fall flat on their faces and wriggle over. To make matters worse, it was horribly windy. They stopped for lunch at 3,350 metres (making sandwiches was out – the meat had frozen solid by this time).

Then they continued their hair-raising climb. But by this time battered Balmat had had enough. He refused to go any further. Somehow, Paccard persuaded him to carry on. Before them loomed a steep icy slope. Plucky Paccard led the way, chipping steps with his ice axe.

Finally, at 6.32 p.m., our two horrible heroes reached the summit. It had taken them 14 long, weary hours. Both men were freezing cold, worn out and suffering from frostbite and snow blindness. But there was no time to rest. There was nowhere to camp on the mountain top so they had to climb straight back down. They reached home at 8 a.m. the following morning and went straight to bed.

But they'd earned their place in the history books . . . and de Saussure's prize.

Earth-shattering fact
Thank your lucky stars you weren't on William Green's expedition up Mount Cook in 1882. He and two guides almost reached the summit when terrible weather forced them back. But on the way down, darkness fell. They were stuck. So they spent the night perched on a tiny ledge, clinging on for dear life. If they'd fallen asleep, they'd have dropped straight off. Simple as that. To stay awake, they sucked sweets and sang hymns. (Luckily, William was a vicar so he knew all the words.)

More mountains to climb

After the thrilling conquest of Mont Blanc, mountaineering never looked back. Climbing became all the rage. Anyone who was anyone joined a climbing club and set off in search of adventure. Peak after peak in the Alps was climbed, one after the other. Then dare-devil climbers set their sights further afield – South America, Africa and Asia. But what about the freakiest mountains of all, the mighty Himalayas? The meanest, moodiest mountains on Earth. Who would reach the top of the world first? The race was on. . .

EXCUSE ME, COMING THROUGH

I DO BEG YOUR PARDON

MAKE WAY THERE

Mystery on the mountain

In 1924, a British expedition of 300 climbers and porters set out to climb Mount Everest. After two years of planning, waiting and organizing, hopes were high. Their route lay up the north side of the mountain in Tibet. For years, Tibet had been out of bounds to foreigners. But in the 1920s, it began to allow foreign climbers in. They seized their chance. Among them was George Leigh Mallory, perhaps the finest and most famous mountaineer of his day. (And the first person to say: "Because it was there.") He'd already been to Everest twice and failed to reach the top. This time he was sure he'd make it. Or die in the attempt. Nobody dared to doubt him. If Mallory couldn't do it, no one could.

Here's how the newspapers of the time might have reported what happened. . .

The Daily Globe
Mount Everest, Tibet

PLUCKY CLIMBERS PERISH ON WORLD'S HIGHEST PEAK

Climbers George Leigh Mallory and Andrew Irvine were feared dead last night, having gone missing on Mount Everest. It is thought that the plucky pair may have plummeted to their deaths, only a few hundred metres from the summit of the world's highest peak.

MALLORY AND IRVINE

The last person to see the two men alive was fellow-climber Noel Odell. He had been setting up camp lower down, ready for Mallory and Irvine's return. Looking up, he spied the two men through a rare break in the clouds, moving well and going strong. It was 12.50 p.m. on 8 June. The men were just 245 metres from the summit.

SO NEAR...

"My eyes became fixed on one tiny black spot silhouetted on a small snow crest beneath a rock step in the ridge," Odell told our reporter. "The black spot moved. Another black spot became apparent and moved up the snow to join the other on the crest. The first then approached the great rock step and shortly emerged on top.

The second did likewise. Then the whole fascinating vision was enveloped in cloud once more."

Mallory and Irvine were never seen again. Mallory, 37, a schoolmaster, had been climbing since his schooldays. Friends and colleagues alike describe him as daring, dashing and one of the greatest climbers of his age. He leaves behind a wife, Ruth, and three young children.

Andrew "Sandy" Irvine, 22, was a promising student at Oxford University. A brilliant sportsman, he and Mallory had become good friends.

Today, tributes poured in to these two brave men, including this one from King George V of England: "They will ever be remembered as fine examples of mountaineers," he said, "ready to risk their lives for their companions and to face dangers on behalf of science and discovery."

A TOP PAIR

We may never know if they made it to the top, or died in the trying.

An icy grave

In March 1999, 75 years after Mallory's death, an American expedition made an astonishing discovery. They were hoping to find Irvine's body. From an ice axe found in 1933 and eyewitness accounts, they thought they knew where he lay. A body was spotted in the snow, lying face down in its icy grave. Was it Irvine? It must be. But the carefully stitched name tags on the tattered clothes told a different story. "G. Mallory", they read. George Mallory. Unbelievably, they had found their hero. With great respect, the climbers buried Mallory's body where it lay, on the mountain he loved.

But the mystery remained. Had Mallory and Irvine made it to the top, 29 years before Tenzing and Hillary? Or had they perished on their way to the summit? Who better to ask than two clued-up climbers. . .

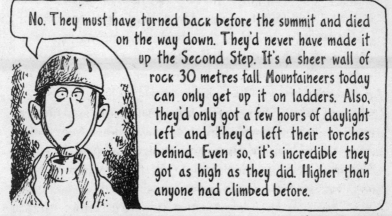

Yes. Noel Odell had excellent eyesight and when he spotted them, they were half-way there. And they had plenty of oxygen left. Besides, it was Mallory's last expedition. He wanted to spend more time at home. It was his life's ambition to climb Mount Everest. For him, it was all or nothing. If only Irvine's camera could be found. A photo of the two men on top of Everest would prove it once and for all.

No. They must have turned back before the summit and died on the way down. They'd never have made it up the Second Step. It's a sheer wall of rock 30 metres tall. Mountaineers today can only get up it on ladders. Also, they'd only got a few hours of daylight left and they'd left their torches behind. Even so, it's incredible they got as high as they did. Higher than anyone had climbed before.

Hmm. Even the experts can't agree. Perhaps this is a mystery that'll never be solved. What do you think?

Freaky peak photo album

Meanwhile, Cliff's been busy with his camera, taking shots of other famous mountaineers. Yes, I know other people's holiday snaps can be horribly boring. But this freaky photo album will have you gripped with excitement. Not convinced? Look on the bright side. It's got to be better than geography homework.

William got into freaky peaks by accident. He was actually looking for goats. He trained as a vet then went to India to set up a shawl-making factory. And the wool for the shawls came from, yes, you've guessed it, goats which lived in the Himalayan mountains. So, in 1812, woolly-headed William set off, disguised as a holy man. (At that time, outsiders weren't very welcome. Without his disguise, he'd have been killed.) Despite being kidnapped and clapped in jail, William finally got his goats. And became the first outsider to explore the mountains. But it was very slow going – the journey took six long years. Still, there was no point bleating about it.

Henriette was the first woman to climb Mont Blanc in 1838. (On her own two feet: in 1808, a young girl was carried to the top to sell food to hungry climbers.) In those days, climbing wasn't considered particularly ladylike and girls had to wear long, tweed skirts. Very respectable but not very practical. (Makes your school uniform look really cool.) But rebellious Henriette cheated and wore a pair of brightly checked trousers under hers. A carrier pigeon brought news of her climb down from the top. Henriette herself toasted her triumph with a glass of ice-cold champagne. Cheers!

Henriette d'Angeville

Isabella Bird
1831 – 1904

ROCK ON

Intrepid Isabella started travelling on doctor's orders. A long journey would do her good, he said. Her family wanted her to get married and settle down but that was much too boring for her. Instead, she set off, alone, for Colorado, USA, to climb the Rocky Mountains. There she fell in love with a no-good bandit called Mountain Jim. Tragically, Jim was later shot dead in a gun fight. In between trips, Isabella wrote best-selling books about her travels. And in case she had any time to spare, she always took her knitting along. At least she never ran out of warm, woolly gloves.

Freaky peak fact file

NAME: The Rocky Mountains (Rockies, for short)

LOCATION: North America (Canada and the USA)

LENGTH: 4,800 km

AGE: about 80 million years old

PEAK TYPE: Fold (see page 24)

PEAKY POINTS:

• The highest peak is Mount Elbert in Colorado at 4,399 m.

• Some of North America's biggest rivers start flowing in the Rockies. They include the Missouri, Rio Grande, Columbia and Colorado, to name a few.

• Many slopes are covered in massive forests of sequoia and redwood trees, the tallest trees in the world. They're cut down for their valuable timber.

• The chinook's a famous local wind that blows in winter. It brings a spell of hot, dry weather, melting the snow. That's why it's nicknamed "snow eater".

CANADA

ATLANTIC OCEAN

ALASKA

USA

THE ROCKIES

MEXICO

SOUTH AMERICA

PACIFIC OCEAN

This is me with Edward Whymper, the first man up the Matterhorn. (Okay, so I'm making the first bit up.) Edward started out as an artist but he gave it up as a job for whymps, sorry, wimps. He climbed this freaky peak on 14 July 1865, beating a team of Italians. (Actually, Edward spotted them below and chucked rocks at them to scare them off.) On the way down, Edward's team was roped together for safety. Then tragedy struck when one man slipped, dragging three others to their deaths. Whymper only survived because the rope broke. It was a very lucky escape.

Tschingel 1865-1879

A life of fetching sticks and chewing slippers was not for this plucky pooch. Between 1868 and 1876, Tschingel the beagle climbed more than 50 major Alpine peaks with her owner, American William Coolidge. And that's a doggy record. To top it all, in 1875, she became the first dog to climb Mont Blanc. On several occasions, Tschingel nearly plunged to her death but was caught by the rope threaded through her collar. But she refused to wear the leather boots doting William had made for her. Woof! Woof!

Reinhold Messner born 1944

Italian climber, Reinhold Messner, is probably the greatest modern-day mountaineer. By the age of 13, he'd already climbed many awesome Alpine peaks. Between 1970 and 1986, he became the first person to climb all 14 of the world's highest peaks (the ones more than 8,000 metres tall). What's more, he was also the first to climb Mount Everest without using oxygen and the first to climb it solo (without ropes or guides). What a guy!

What goes up, must come down

You know the saying "What goes up, must come down"?
Well, generally speaking it's true. Picture the scene . . .
you've dragged yourself up your freaky peak, you've soaked
in the scenery and it's time to head down. Easier said than
done. Here are five way-out ways to reach rock bottom. Can
you tell which ones are too risky to be real?

1) SKIING...

2) HANG-GLIDING...

3) CANOEING...

4) ZIP WIRING...

5) GLISSADING...

98

Answers: Believe it or not, all of these are true. What's more, they've all been tried and tested. . .

1 Every year, thousands of people take to the hills to experience the thrills and spills of skiing. They catch the lift up, then ski back down. For fun, apparently. But downhill skiing's a serious sport – you'd have to be seriously barmy to do it. The world's top skiiers hurtle downhill at staggering speeds of almost 250 kilometres per hour. That's as fast as a high-speed train. Whoosh!

2 In the 1980s, two French climbers, Boivin and Marchal, came down from the summit of Mount Aconcagua, not on foot . . . but by hang-glider! They landed about half-way down the mountain, having soared in the air for 20 minutes. Lucky they didn't get carried away.

3 In 1976, two British canoeists, Mike Jones and Mike Hopkinson, canoed down the Dudh Kosi River on Mount Everest. This high-rise river flows from an icy lake more than 5,000 metres up on the Khumbu Icefall. Blocks of ice the size of houses regularly break off this ghastly glacier and crash into the river below.

4 Get this. A person slides down a rope from the top of a cliff . . . by his or her ankle. Or sitting on a bicycle. Unbelievably some freaky people do this for a thrill. WARNING: this is a horribly dangerous thing to do. Never, ever try it.

5 Glissading comes from a French word for sliding. It means slipping and sliding down a steep icy slope on your feet . . . or on your bum. The fastest descent of Mount Everest was made in 1986. Two climbers glissaded down 2,500 metres on their bottoms. When they wanted to stop, they used their ice axes as brakes. Their slide took 3.5 hours. Painful!

Could you be a top mountaineer? Are you daring enough to climb Mount Everest? If you like living on the edge, hurry into the next chapter for the adventure of a lifetime. But if all this excitement's left you exhausted, don't freak out. If your teacher's so keen on freaky peak field trips, why not send her instead?

·P·E·A·K··S·U·R·V·I·V·A·L·

Freaky peaks are perilous places to be. But if your teacher's dead set on getting to the top, has she really got what it takes to be a top mountaineer? Is she fighting fit? Cool in a crisis? Does she have a good head for heights? Is she breath-takingly brave and horribly hardy? Where she's going, she'll need to be. Mountaineering's not for the faint-hearted. Is she still keen to go? Is she stark staring bonkers? Luckily she'll have Cliff to show her the ropes. . .

Are you brave enough to climb Mount Everest?

What you need:

- a very large mountain
- lots of posh climbing clothes

> If you're climbing a freaky peak, you need to dress for the part. There's no point setting off up Mount Everest in jeans and a T-shirt, however cool you think you look. You need clothes that'll protect you from the cold and wind, otherwise you'll freeze to death. Don't worry, there's lots of trendy kit around to keep you snug as a bug. Look over the page to see me modelling the latest red-hot look in groovy climbing gear: It's what every modern mountaineer's wearing. . .

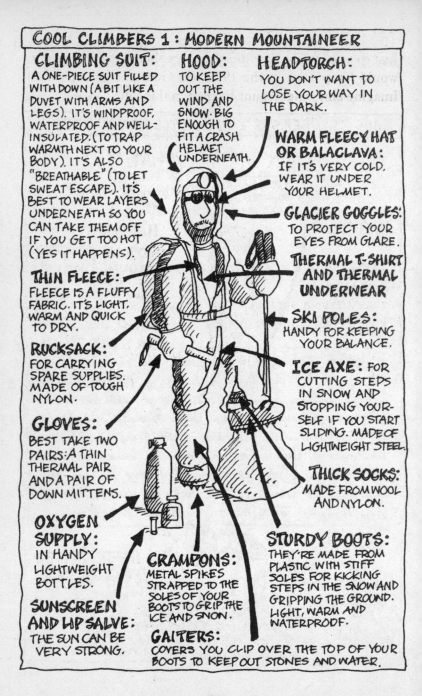

CLIMBING SUIT:
A ONE-PIECE SUIT FILLED WITH DOWN (A BIT LIKE A DUVET WITH ARMS AND LEGS). IT'S WINDPROOF, WATERPROOF AND WELL-INSULATED. (TO TRAP WARMTH NEXT TO YOUR BODY). IT'S ALSO "BREATHABLE" (TO LET SWEAT ESCAPE). IT'S BEST TO WEAR LAYERS UNDERNEATH SO YOU CAN TAKE THEM OFF IF YOU GET TOO HOT (YES IT HAPPENS).

HOOD:
TO KEEP OUT THE WIND AND SNOW. BIG ENOUGH TO FIT A CRASH HELMET UNDERNEATH.

HEADTORCH:
YOU DON'T WANT TO LOSE YOUR WAY IN THE DARK.

WARM FLEECY HAT OR BALACLAVA:
IF IT'S VERY COLD, WEAR IT UNDER YOUR HELMET.

GLACIER GOGGLES:
TO PROTECT YOUR EYES FROM GLARE.

THERMAL T-SHIRT AND THERMAL UNDERWEAR

THIN FLEECE:
FLEECE IS A FLUFFY FABRIC. IT'S LIGHT, WARM AND QUICK TO DRY.

SKI POLES:
HANDY FOR KEEPING YOUR BALANCE.

RUCKSACK:
FOR CARRYING SPARE SUPPLIES. MADE OF TOUGH NYLON.

ICE AXE: FOR CUTTING STEPS IN SNOW AND STOPPING YOURSELF IF YOU START SLIDING. MADE OF LIGHTWEIGHT STEEL.

GLOVES:
BEST TAKE TWO PAIRS: A THIN THERMAL PAIR AND A PAIR OF DOWN MITTENS.

THICK SOCKS:
MADE FROM WOOL AND NYLON.

OXYGEN SUPPLY:
IN HANDY LIGHTWEIGHT BOTTLES.

CRAMPONS:
METAL SPIKES STRAPPED TO THE SOLES OF YOUR BOOTS TO GRIP THE ICE AND SNOW.

STURDY BOOTS:
THEY'RE MADE FROM PLASTIC WITH STIFF SOLES FOR KICKING STEPS IN THE SNOW AND GRIPPING THE GROUND. LIGHT, WARM AND WATERPROOF.

SUNSCREEN AND LIP SALVE:
THE SUN CAN BE VERY STRONG.

GAITERS:
COVERS YOU CLIP OVER THE TOP OF YOUR BOOTS TO KEEP OUT STONES AND WATER.

Just so you realize how lucky you are, here's what a climber would have worn in the 1920s (in George Mallory's day). Imagine climbing Mount Everest in this lot. . .

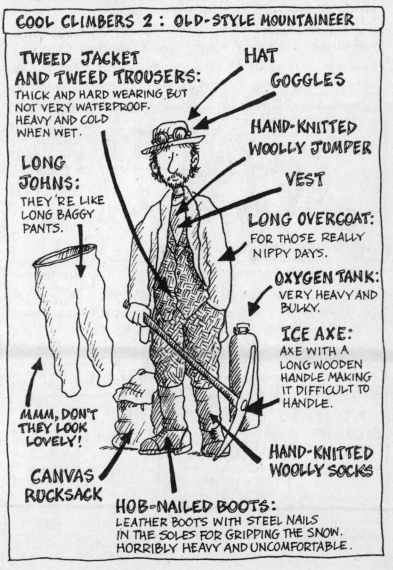

COOL CLIMBERS 2 : OLD-STYLE MOUNTAINEER

TWEED JACKET AND TWEED TROUSERS: THICK AND HARD WEARING BUT NOT VERY WATERPROOF. HEAVY AND COLD WHEN WET.

HAT

GOGGLES

HAND-KNITTED WOOLLY JUMPER

VEST

LONG JOHNS: THEY'RE LIKE LONG BAGGY PANTS.

LONG OVERCOAT: FOR THOSE REALLY NIPPY DAYS.

OXYGEN TANK: VERY HEAVY AND BULKY.

ICE AXE: AXE WITH A LONG WOODEN HANDLE MAKING IT DIFFICULT TO HANDLE.

MMM, DON'T THEY LOOK LOVELY!

HAND-KNITTED WOOLLY SOCKS

CANVAS RUCKSACK

HOB-NAILED BOOTS: LEATHER BOOTS WITH STEEL NAILS IN THE SOLES FOR GRIPPING THE SNOW. HORRIBLY HEAVY AND UNCOMFORTABLE.

- reliable ropes: you might need to rope on to another person to cross a gruesome glacier. Or to go up a steep slope. So it's vital your rope's super-strong, and not about to break. Modern ropes are made of tough nylon. They're light, hardwearing and waterproof. (In the olden days, ropes were made from plant fibres. They froze when they got wet, making them hard to hold on to.) Some bits of Mount Everest have fixed ropes (they're always left in place). You clip or tie yourself on, then climb up.

- tent: you need a tent that's light to carry, strong and waterproof. Light metal tent poles are best. They'll bend a bit in high winds, so your tent doesn't blow away. Practise pitching your tent before you go. You won't have time to read the instructions on the mountain.

- sleeping bag

- food and drink: you'll need plenty to eat and drink. Climbing uses up loads of energy. Here's what you might eat on a typical day:

Today's Menu

Breakfast:
Cereal, Biscuits
Fruit

Lunch:
Bread, Cheese,
Salami, Crackers, Nuts,
High-Energy Bar

Dinner:
Soup,
Noodles or Pasta,
Mashed Potatoes,
Fish or Meat,
Biscuits, Fruit

Drinks:
Tea, Coffee, Cocoa,
High-Energy Drinks
Milk (Powdered)
Water

- a cooking stove, pots, cup, spoon and bowl

What you do:

1 Plan your route. The most popular route's up the South Face (that's the way Tenzing and Hillary went). You set up higher and higher camps until you reach the top. Hopefully. Each camp's stocked with spare supplies, equipment and climbers to back you up. It's a long, rocky road to get to the top. In case you get lost, here's a handy map to help you:

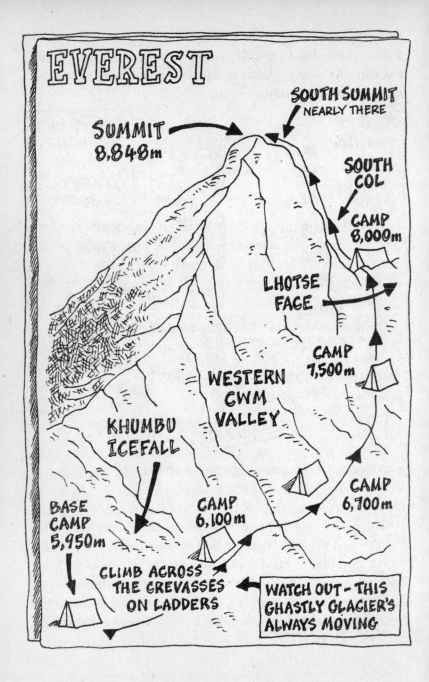

2 Ask permission. You'll need a permit to climb Mount Everest. At about £45,000, they're pretty pricey so start saving your pocket money now.

YOU'RE TAKING A LOT OF GEAR!

THIS IS JUST THE MONEY FOR MY CLIMBING PERMIT!

The best time to go is mid–May when the weather's good. Usually. Avoid the summer – you'll be swept away by the monsoon rains. The trouble is, peaky weather can change in a flash, catching you unawares. Always check the weather forecast before you set out.

TODAY, MOUNT EVEREST WILL HAVE SUNSHINE, THEN RAIN, A BIT OF SNOW, LIGHT WINDS, MEDIUM WINDS, STRONG WINDS, FUNNY SMELLING WINDS! ANOTHER DOLLOP OF SNOW, MORE SUNSHINE, THEN RAIN...

3 Get into training. You'll need to be fighting fit to climb Mount Everest. So if you're always trying to get out of games, you might want to give up now. A good way to get fit is to run up and down stairs, carrying a rucksack full of bricks. You'd better get used to it because you'll be lugging around loads of heavy gear. Running, swimming and weight training are also brilliant for building up your strength.

4 Choose your team. An expedition needs tonnes of gear just to keep it going – first you have to lug it to base camp, then higher and higher up. There's no way you can carry it all (even with all that weight training), so you'll have to hire some Sherpa porters and yaks to help you out. About 100 should do. Some Sherpas specialize in climbing high up – you can rely on them when the going gets really tough.

5 Get going. There's no time to lose. It will take you weeks to reach base camp. And even then, you're only half-way there. Don't forget to say your prayers before you set off to soften up the mountain gods. You're going to need all the help you can get. . . Good luck!

Teacher teaser

Tie your teacher up in knots with this harmless-sounding question. Put up your hand, smile, and say:

PLEASE, SIR THERE'S AN ALPINE BUTTERFLY IN SIMPKIN'S HAIR. SHALL I CATCH IT AND PUT IT OUT THE WINDOW?

Does your teacher tell you to get knotted?

Answer: Of course not. Teachers are much too polite. But you're nearer the truth than you think. An Alpine butterfly isn't an insect that flutters about or lands on people's hair, it's a type of knot. And it's horribly useful in climbing. You use it to tie yourself to a rope so you don't fall. Here's how you do it:

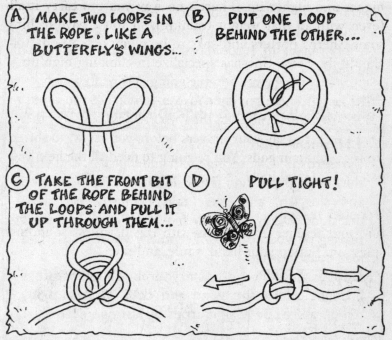

A) MAKE TWO LOOPS IN THE ROPE, LIKE A BUTTERFLY'S WINGS...

B) PUT ONE LOOP BEHIND THE OTHER...

C) TAKE THE FRONT BIT OF THE ROPE BEHIND THE LOOPS AND PULL IT UP THROUGH THEM...

D) PULL TIGHT!

Got all that? Good. You never know when you might need it.

HORRIBLE HEALTH WARNING

Mountains can be dangerous. More than 675 people have climbed Mount Everest . . . and more than 160 never made it back down. If your teacher's serious about climbing mountains, make sure she goes to an expert for help. If she runs into trouble, she could call base camp on a solar-powered or satellite phone. Most expeditions carry them. Then if someone's badly injured, a rescue helicopter can be called in. But it can only land at base camp. Weather permitting. . .

Feeling peaky?

There are plenty of other horrible hazards waiting to freak you out on the mountainside. Don't leave home without your copy of the *Freaky Peak First Aid Manual*. Better still, read it before you set off. It could make the difference between life and death.

FREAKY PEAK FIRST AID MANUAL

1 Hypothermia

Symptoms: Chattering teeth and blue lips. You start shivering slowly, then faster and faster. You feel tired and sluggish, and can't talk properly, or make decisions. Oddly, you may feel very warm and start tearing off your clothes. Eventually you collapse and lose consciousness.

Cause: A sudden drop in your body temperature brought on by the wind and cold. Normal body temperature's 37°C. If it drops by just two degrees, it can be fatal.

Treatment: Wrap up warm and drink plenty of fluids to keep your circulation flowing. Eat plenty of sugary food for energy.

2 Dehydration

Symptoms: You feel thirsty, sleepy and sick. Then you get a headache. You can't walk or talk properly, and you don't know where you are. Can be fatal.

Cause: You lose loads of water as sweat as you climb. And the dry mountain air makes things worse.

Treatment: Drink plenty of water, even if you don't feel like it. If you wait until you feel thirsty, it may be too late. Whatever you do, don't eat the snow. It'll cool your body down even further. To tell if you're dehydrated, look at the colour of your pee. If it's light yellow, you're fine. If it's dark brown, you're in trouble.

WHAT HAPPENS WHEN IT'S PURPLE?

3 Snow blindness

Symptoms: Your eyes start to sting, then you see everything in shades of reddish pink. It's as if your eyes are full of gritty sand. Then you go blind for hours, or even days.

Cause: The glare of the sun's rays reflected from the ice or snow.

Treatment: Get into a dark place and cover your eyes with a damp, cooling cloth. Don't rub your eyes.

Better still, wear glacier goggles or strong sunglasses to protect your eyes from the glare, even when it's foggy.

STILL HAVING TROUBLE WITH YOUR EYES?

4 Frostbite

Symptoms: Attacks your fingers, feet, ears and nose. First they feel prickly, then numb. Later they turn red, swollen and blistery. Then they turn black and drop off.

Cause: Your skin and flesh get so cold, they freeze solid and die. Mild frostbite is called frostnip.

Treatment: Try to thaw out the frozen bits. Warning: this will be painful. Pull faces to stop frostbite freezing your nose. As a last resort, your fingers and toes may have to be amputated (cut off). Horrible.

5 Mountain sickness

Symptoms: Feels like a bad dose of flu, with headaches, sickness and loss of appetite. You feel tired but you can't go to sleep. You get a hacking cough and find it hard to breathe. You might even start seeing things.

Cause: Lack of oxygen high up. The trouble is, it can strike without warning once you're about 2,500 metres up. One minute you're feeling fine, the next you're hacking your guts up.

Treatment: Get down the mountain. Otherwise you could die. Or get into a Gamow bag (it's like a long, nylon tube you blow up with a pump). It'll release the pressure on your lungs. Then you can climb down.

Killer snows

Snow. You might think it's nice, white, fluffy stuff you see on Christmas cards. Think again. Believe it or not, snow can be a killer. Without any warning, thousands of tonnes of the stuff can roar down a mountain in an awful, awesome avalanche, sweeping away everything in its path – trees, people, cars, even whole villages. There's no escape from the dreaded white death, as this terrifying true story shows. . .

Galtur, Austria, 23 February 1999

Just before 4 p.m. on 23 February 1999, disaster hit Galtur in the Austrian Alps. The sleepy village, a popular skiing resort, was devastated by the worst avalanche to hit the region in 30 years. Villagers and visitors looked on helplessly as a massive wall of snow buried the village, bulldozering trees, houses and cars out of its way. Thirty-one people died; many more were badly injured. And half of Galtur was smashed into pieces. One survivor described the awful moment when the avalanche struck:

> We had just gone into our hotel room when suddenly everything went black. There was no sound at all. Then something smacked against the window like a giant shockwave. Then you heard it hitting the other side of the hotel.

There had been no warning so people had only a few seconds to get out of the way. For some, there was no escape. Anyone buried under the snow stood only a very slim chance of survival. The only sign of the coming catastrophe was a thunderous roar as the vast slab of snow suddenly broke free and came crashing down the mountain. Besides, Galtur stood about 200 metres away from the base of the mountain so people thought it was safely out of reach of an avalanche. Small avalanches were a common sight but they usually trickled out long before they reached the village. Elsewhere in the valley, snow fences had been built across the slopes to slow the pace of any falling snow. But not around Galtur. No one thought they were needed there. No one expected the big one.

Scientists believed the tragedy was caused by freak winter weather in the Alps – some of the worst weather in living memory. In February alone, a record-breaking four metres of snow had fallen. Strong winds whipped the snow into dangerous drifts, pointing ominously towards Galtur. At any time, the snow could give way, with terrible consequences. It was a disaster waiting to happen. To make matters worse, roads and air links to Galtur had been closed for five days because of the atrocious weather. By the time the rescue teams finally arrived, some people had been buried in snow for 16 hours. Incredibly, 40 people were still pulled out alive. Against all the odds.

So what on Earth are avalanches? And how do these silent killers strike?

Some awful avalanche facts

1 An avalanche is a mass of mountain snow that suddenly breaks loose and crashes downhill. Galtur was hit by a "powder" avalanche. That's the type where tonnes of soft, powdery snow falls on to an icy layer. Then cracks begin to appear in the ice making the soft snow on top unstable – so unstable it suddenly starts to slip and slide.

2 For the snow to slide, it needs to be heavy enough to overcome friction (that's the freaky force that holds it to the rock). Then gravity does the rest. In Galtur, an astonishing 17,000 tonnes of snow hurtled down the mountainside. Which was bad enough. But by the time the avalanche hit

the village, it had picked up so much snow it had doubled in size. Imagine the size of that snowball!

3 Watch out if you're skiing. A number of things can trigger off a slide, including the weight of a single skier. Unfortunately, the peak avalanche season's January to March: the perfect time for skiing. The slamming of a car door can do the trick. Or even yodelling. Yes, yodelling. You know, that strange, high-pitched warbling sound? Well, in some Swiss mountain villages, yodelling is banned in spring when the avalanche risk is greatest. And village children aren't allowed to shout or sing either. Sounds a bit like a geography lesson.

4 Some avalanches move at high speeds of up to 320 kilometres an hour. Whoosh! That's as fast as a racing car. And they get faster the further they flow. The Galtur avalanche was going so fast, it took two whole minutes to come to a standstill. Doesn't sound much but that only gave people a measly 10 to 20 seconds to escape. Not long enough.

5 Believe it or not, in the First World War, avalanches were used as deadly weapons. Austrian and Italian troops fighting in the Alps aimed their fire at the mountain tops instead of at each other, triggering off loads of lethal avalanches. In 1916, 80,000 soldiers were killed in this way. In a single day!

6 Scientists are working hard to find a way to forecast when and where avalanches will strike next, so that a warning can be given. In the Alps, there are mini weather stations on each mountain top, measuring things like temperature, snowfall and rainfall. All crucial clues to avalanches. The scientists feed this data into computers and get them to come up with a forecast. So how good are they? The good news is they're getting better all the time. The bad news is it's not an exact science. You can't give a forecast for a particular valley, only for a whole region. And avalanches are horribly fickle.

7 So can anything stop an avalanche in its tracks? Well, various things have been tried. On some freaky peaks, steel fences are built across the slopes to hold the snow back. And houses are avalanche-proofed, with tough concrete walls and no doors or windows on the avalanche side. From time to time, experts deliberately use explosives to trigger off smallish slides. This helps avoid a dangerous build-up of snow. Sounds horribly risky, but it works. But the terrible truth is, once the snow gets flowing, there's no way on Earth you're going to get it to stop.

Cliff's top tips for avalanche safety

So if you're unlucky enough to be caught in an avalanche, what on Earth can you do? Unfortunately, your chances of survival are pretty slim. Around the world, avalanches kill about 200 people a year. Most suffocate to death as the snow sets solid around them, like icy concrete. Very nasty. But don't freak out. If a sinister snow slide's heading your way, try to remember these life-saving tips:

If you're caught in an avalanche. . .

- As the avalanche starts, try to get behind a shelter like a rock or a tree.
- Close your mouth so you don't swallow too much snow. And cover your nose with your hands. This will give you a bit of breathing space under the snow.
- Try to stay upright by waving your arms as if you're swimming. It might sound silly but it could save your life.

- When the snow stops, find out which way up you are by spitting. If the spit dribbles down your chin, you're upright. If it dribbles across your face, you're upside-down. If you can move, try to dig yourself out. In the opposite direction to the spit.

- Always carry a radio transceiver. It's a gadget you wear around your neck which will beep loudly so rescuers can find you under the snow.

If you're searching for someone. . .

- Switch your transceiver to receive mode. Then you'll be able to pick up any signals for help.

- Search the area carefully for any clues. Use a long stick, called a snow probe, to prod the snow (gently) in case there's a body buried below.

- Take the dog for a walk. Dogs are brilliant at sniffing out victims because their noses are so sensitive. Forget posh high-tech equipment – dogs are by far the best.

- When you find someone, start digging them out straight away. There's no time to lose. Even after half an hour, most victims are dead. Uncover their mouth first so they can breathe. Then get them off the mountain, fast.

Freaky, isn't it? But DON'T PANIC. Remember, you're much more likely to be excused geography homework for the rest of your schooldays than be swept away by an avalanche. And how likely is that?

But never mind about climbing mountains because they are there. If horrible humans don't mend their ways, they might not be there much longer...

PEAK CONDITION

Despite all the dangers, it's official. Horrible humans are hooked on hills. But do freaky peaks like having them there? Or does all that tramping take its toll? Mountains might look as though they'll last for ever, but don't be fooled. They're far more fragile than they appear. Time to head off for Africa and freaky Mount Kilimanjaro. . .

Trouble on the mountain

Local Chagga people have lived on the slopes of Mount Kilimanjaro for hundreds of years. They believe the mountain's holy and treat it with great respect. After all, they say, you can't get closer to heaven than that. But it's more than just a mountain – its bubbling springs provide the Chagga with water for drinking and growing crops. Without it, they couldn't survive. But today the mountain's in grave danger. And with it the Chagga's traditional way of life.

In 1970, Kilimanjaro was turned into a national park to protect its stunning scenery. Thousands of tourists visit Tanzania each year for the thrill of climbing this freaky peak. It's a six-day hike to the top. The tourists bring in much-needed money and many of the Chagga get work as porters and guides. So far, so good. Trouble is, with around 18,000 hikers a year, not to mention 54,000 porters and guides, peaky Kilimanjaro is feeling the strain.

121

With so many climbers camping on the mountain, huge patches of forest have been cleared for firewood. And it only takes one careless spark from a camp fire to spark off a disastrous forest fire, leaving thousands of acres of mountain in ashes. It can take years and years for the trees to grow back again.

What's more, it's changing the lives of the Chagga too. They're being forced off their mountain, to live on the dry, dusty plains below. They used to hunt for food and graze their animals on the hillside. But they're not allowed to do this any more. Sadly, many are turning their backs on the mountain. Many people are very poor. So they cut down rare trees in the forest and sell the valuable wood for money. With fewer trees, the forests can't store water. Instead of seeping underground, any rain simply washes away. So there aren't as many mountain springs (you get these where underground water bubbles up to the surface), and the rivers are drying up. Which means people suffer even more because they don't have enough water for drinking and growing crops. It's a horribly vicious circle.

People are trying to put things right. They're planting more trees and limiting the number of trekkers. And children are learning to love the mountain as part of their geography lessons at school. Will it work? It's too early to say for sure. But it's worth it to save this breath-taking peak from going rapidly downhill.

Freaky peak fact file

NAME: Mount Kilimanjaro

LOCATION: Tanzania, Africa

HEIGHT: 5,895 metres

AGE: 500-300,000 years old

PEAK TYPE: Volcano (see page 27)

PEAKY POINTS:

• Kilimanjaro's the highest peak in Africa. It towers above the plains all around.

• Its name means "Shining Mountain" or "Mountain of Spring Water" in the local language.

• It's actually three freaky peaks joined together. There's Kibo, the highest, Mawenzi and Shira. Kibo's been dormant (sleeping) for the last 200 years.

• In 100 years' time, the great glaciers on Kibo could be gone for good. It's because the world's weather is getting warmer. They've already shrunk by half in the last century.

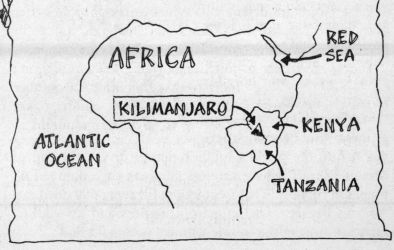

HORRIBLE HEALTH WARNING

It's not just Kilimanjaro that's under pressure. Things look bleak in the Himalayas too. Why? In Nepal so many trees have been chopped down for firewood, many slopes have been stripped bare. And without any tree roots to cement the soil together, it's easily washed away. Apart from the danger of serious landslides, the soil's causing problems by silting up the mountain rivers. This causes fatal flooding further downstream.

High-rise rubbish

Mountaineers have a saying: when you climb a mountain, any mountain, don't leave anything but footprints behind. Sensible advice. Freaky peaks are horribly sensitive places. The last thing they need is you making a mess. But guess where you'll find the world's highest junkyard? On the top of Mount Everest, where careless climbers have dumped 60 tonnes of rubbish. That's enough to fill about 600 dustbins. And it's having a fatal effect on the peak and its wildlife. Here are some of the freakiest things you might find. . .

Oxygen bottles (used)

Old tents and tent poles

Toilet paper (used)

Cardboard boxes

Plastic bags

Cereal packets

Tins, Jars and glass bottles

Old syringes and needles

Baseball bats and frisbees

Gas cylinders (for cooking stoves)

A crashed helicopter

Dead bodies (some still clipped onto ropes) it's true!

Peak protection

Mountains are certainly in a bit of a mess but things aren't all gloom and doom. Campaigns are underway to spring clean the mountains. Why not start up one of your own? If you find yourself up a freaky peak, do your bit to keep it in peak condition. Don't know where to start? Over the page are a few simple rules to follow:

1 If you're making a fire, use as little wood as possible. And put the fire out properly afterwards.

2 Burn or bury any litter that'll rot away (like paper and, yes, dead bodies). Pack the rest up and take it home. Today, if you drop litter on Mount Everest, you're in for a hefty fine.

3 Keep mountain streams sparkling clean. After all, they're used for drinking water. So don't wash your dishes in a stream or use it as a toilet. Dirty water can spread deadly diseases.

4 Don't pick the flowers or dig up the plants. And don't disturb the animals. Things are tough enough for peaky wildlife without you making it worse.

5 And finally . . . 2002 is officially the International Year of Mountains. So why not go and give a hill a hug. Go on, nobody's looking. . .

A peaky future?

So what does the future hold for freaky peaks? Nobody really knows. But one thing's for certain: mountains will carry on growing and shrinking. Little by little, every year. And there's nothing anyone can do about it. As the Earth's pushy plates continue to move, it'll be goodbye to many of the peaks we know. Sounds freaky. But it won't happen overnight. As you know, mountain building takes millions and millions of years. (Quite soon in geographical time but not soon enough to get you out of your field trip.) At the same time, brand-new mountains are always being born. And, experts reckon, these freaky peaks could grow even higher than sky-scraping Mount Everest. Now *that's* amazing.

If you're interested in finding out more about freaky peaks, here are some web sites you can visit.

www.thebmc.co.uk/gripped
The British Mountaineering Council's magazine for young people. Packed with features, events and contacts for young climbers.

www.mnteverest.net
Statistics, quotes and information about planning expeditions to Mount Everest.

www.everestnews.com/
More news from the top of the world, with weather reports and information about expeditions in progress.

library.advanced.org/10131
This site focuses on the Himalayas and is full of freaky facts about their history, geology and the dangers facing them from climbers and pollution.

sung3.ifsi.rm.cnr.it/dargaud/Climbing
A climber's own site with reports of his own climbing expeditions around the world, with fabulous photos.

www.americas-roof.com/
This site covers every high mountain right across the USA and gives loads of details about how to hike up one.